Intangible Inheritance

A Lyrical Memoir

2nd Edition

by

Ellen Li Juan

David Juan M.D. (Revised)

DORRANCE
PUBLISHING CO
EST. 1920
PITTSBURGH, PENNSYLVANIA 15238

Dorrance Publishing Co
585 Alpha Drive
Pittsburgh, PA 15238
Visit our website at www.dorrancebookstore.com

ISBN: 979-8-88812-183-2
eISBN: 979-8-88812-683-7

CONTENTS

To
All True Men of God

Dearest Abby & Michael,

A special "intangible inheritance" for you to treasure

Love Soma

8/17/25

Key Dates of Li Yuanmo

1871 – born in Hubei Province, China

1876 – his mother passed away when he was 5 years old

1878 – started schooling at 7 years old

1899 – founded Gruangyi School in Anhui, Wuhu

1907 – visited Japan attending world Christian Youth Meeting at 36 years old

1915-1921 – served in Episcopal Church in Jiangxi Province, China

1922 – moved to Wuhu

1944 – one son and one daughter passed away within 4 months; fell down at son's funeral and has needed walking stick since then

1948 – took train from Wuhu to Nanjing (capitol city of China back then) to visit the author and her family with three children and her family with three children

1951 – died at 81 years old

PREFACE

THE BIRTH OF THIS BOOK IS THE RESULT OF A spontaneous outflowing of the precious sentiments of love and admiration from the depths of my heart. The inner pushing has been so irresistible and impulsive that my hand was finally given courage to write in two languages, Chinese and English, the beautiful traces that my father has unconsciously yet incessantly embroidered on the pattern of my life.

To write about one's own parent sounds very personal, for everyone has a father and mother. What, then, is the significant bearing of my father's life experiences upon those of other nations, of other races? This is the key question that had to be answered within the writer's heart before the book was written. The same question, I anticipate, will puzzle every reader, too, until he finds the answer through reading it.

The content of the book is the content of a man's real life expressed in the form of a lyrical memoir. It is not a story drawn from the imagination. Neither is it the writer's intention to stress the biblical precepts in order to magnify the philosophy of life or to exalt the social value of the man concerned.

The book may stir in the minds and hearts of readers some charming ripples, curling around as they flow tranquil stream; it may help them to construct a new vision of the world. Perhaps the book will enter a reader's life at a crucial moment, when he feels bored, pessimistic, or restless because of current realities. If this book might serve as a compass to reorientate one's view of life, to reanimate one's enthusiasm for pursuing a noble and meaningful cause, or to refill a weary soul with vitality, then it would abundantly reap what it has sown.

I extend my deepest appreciation and gratitude to my friends, colleagues, and students in Hong Kong, in Formosa, and in the United States who have given me continuous encouragement and moral support. I am particularly indebted to my former teacher in English Literature, Professor Harold Shadick, former head of the English Department of Yenching University, now professor at Cornell University, for giving me valuable advice and suggestions, and to Dr. James K. C. Juan, my husband, for his many-sided assistance and deep interest in my writing, and to Mr. George Tseng, of Baylor University, for his technical help. It is due to the combined effort of men and the grace of God that my desire to write.

May 15, 1960
Palo Alto, CA   ELLEN LI JUAN

ACKNOWLEDGEMENTS

My mother wrote this book in 1960, almost 70 years ago and unfortunately passed in 1965 from liver cancer. During this time, there is a meteoric explosion of knowledge. Steve Jobs and Bill Gates ushered in the digital age whereas Drs James Watson, Francis Crick, Francis Collins the age of human genome. In general, people are living a better life with an increasing amount of material goods to satisfy the sensual needs of the moment. Everyone has a smart phone in their hand capable of transmitting words, photos and videos instantaneously to friends anywhere on earth. Ironically, this modern technological advancement negatively impacted communication between human beings. Thus, it is not surprising that the human heart is more restless as witnessed by increase in mood disorders, suicide rate, opioid epidemic. In St. Augustine Confessions he wrote this famous quote:

"You have made us for yourself, O Lord, and our heart is restless until it rests in you."

My grandfather, Reverend Li Yuan Mo was such a person who did not amass material goods while alive but found true peace and joy because his heart rested in God, the creator of heaven and earth. Moreover, he made sure that his children and grandchildren know and trust the same God he did. Indeed, we are the benefactors of his Intangible Inheritance. In this edition, I have added maps of the cities mentioned in the book. I thought that adding photos relevant to my grandfather would be of interest to the reader.

I would like to thank the following individuals:

* Rosaline Y. Negrete, my daughter, for her help with editing and proofreading
* Li Wei-yong, my great grand cousin, for supplying the valuable photos
* May Chen, my sister, for her encouragement and support
* Dorrance Publishing

FOREWORD

Intangible Inheritance: A Lyrical Memoir is a book like no other and absolutely true to its title. Try as one might, the reader attempts in vain to put his arms around the subject of this biography and is never quite able to do so. It is beautifully written and at the same time articulately expressed with deep emotion. It is the biography of her father by Ellen Li Juan which needs to be read by all, especially by the next generation. This tribute will not only provide encouragement but point the way of finding true meaning in life.

Y.M. Lee was born in 1871, son of a poor farmer, who rose to become a powerful "spiritual" farmer in China. His story keeps you riveted from the very beginning of his life through the following eight decades. It brought back to me memories of old China, although our lives only overlapped about twenty years. Three things struck me about his life: The personal example of his life, the guidance he provided for others through his teaching ministry, and his love for the Word of God.

He lost his mother at age 5 and work at a young age became his norm. Suffering and testing were part and parcel of his maturing process. This became a molding experience for him, particularly after he became a follower of Christ. It was here that a strength of character surfaced, which puts him right in line with the heroes of faith mentioned in Hebrews 11.

There was an utter commitment to personal discipline, integrity and perseverance that stands alone, especially in our day and age. It reminded me of the apostle Paul's advice to young Timothy when he said: "Be diligent in these matters; give yourself wholly to them, so that everyone may see your progress. Watch your life and doctrine closely. Persevere in them, because if you do, you will save both yourself and your hearers." (I Tim. 4:15,16). Y.M. Lee was that kind of a man and set a powerful example for all who follow in his trail.

I was blessed reading this book and highly recommend it to all who have a deep desire to follow Jesus. You will be blessed as well!

Dr. Hans M. Wilhelm

China-born, German-American missionary/pastor on five continents

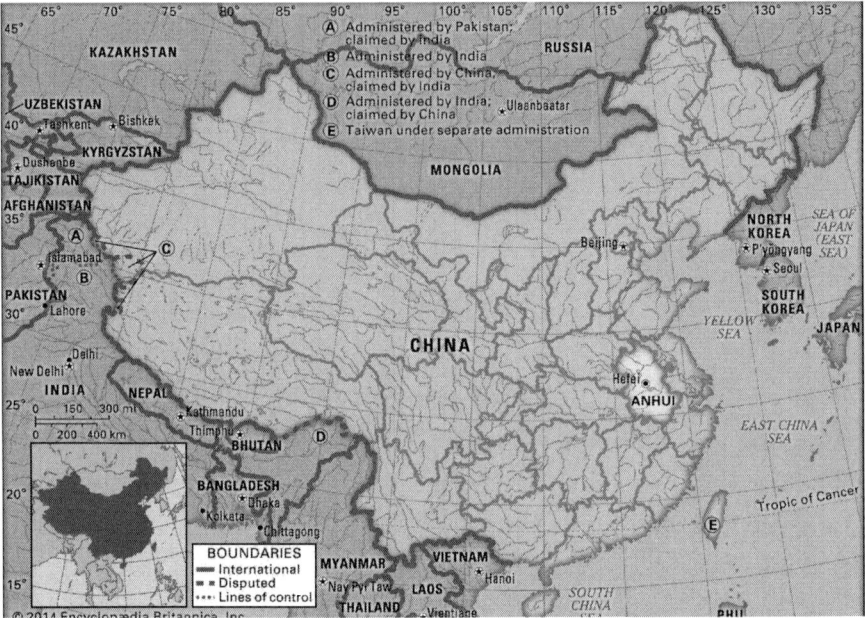

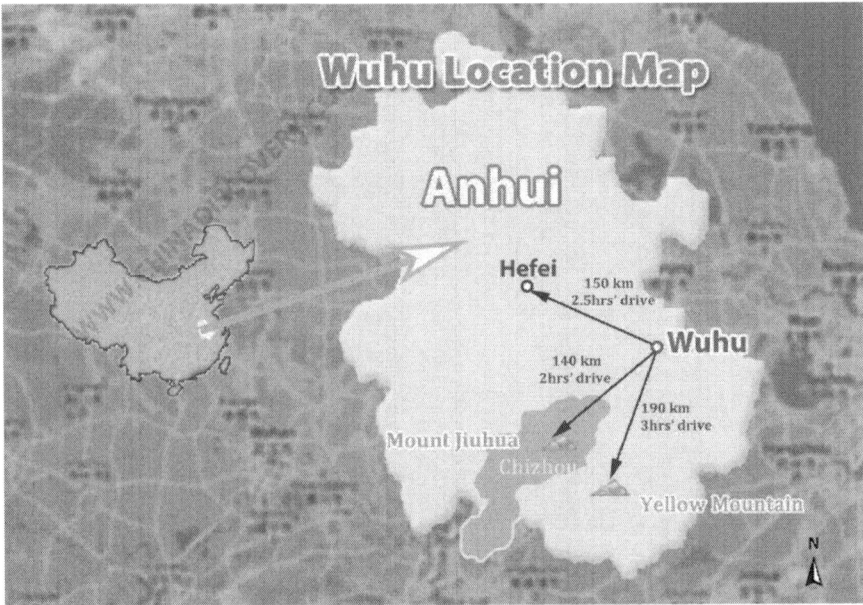

Wuhu Location Map

Anhui

Hefei
150 km
2.5hrs' drive

Wuhu

140 km
2hrs' drive

190 km
3hrs' drive

Mount Jiuhua
Chizhou

Yellow Mountain

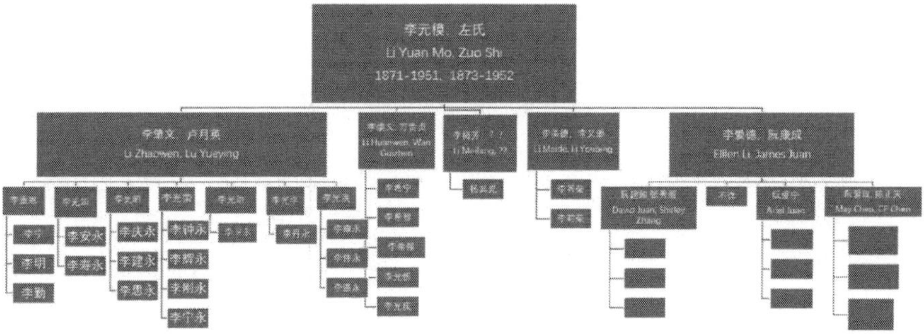
李元模、左氏
Li Yuan Mo, Zuo Shi
1871-1951, 1873-1952
Li Zhaowen, Lu Yueying
Ellen Li, James Juan
李明
李勤
李安永
李建永
李刚永
David Juan, Shirley Zhang
May Chen, CF Chen

TOUCHING HYMN

1

THE CHURCH BELL CHIMES GOD'S DEVOUT INTO HIS house every Sunday. Among these Christians I can usually be found, calmly sitting in a preferred corner of the church. On one Sunday, as I was holding the Universal Hymn Book, I seemed to be deeply touched by the announcement of the minister:

"Please sing hymn number 352, 'I Am a Pilgrim Here.'"

The melodious tune, played by the skillful fingers of the organist, filled the entire church. The congregation sang it in Chinese. I felt overwhelmed both with grief and pride by this beautiful hymn. Matching the holy music, the verses, which were written with deep religious sentiment, vibrated through the solemn air and seemed to reach into everyone's consciousness. Every human heart responds differently to the tune, but mine is flooded with many sweet and imperishable memories, because the writer of this hymn was my beloved father, a Christian pioneer, a spiritual reformer, a striker of the bell of vigilance for our Lord for nearly sixty years of his life.

When I sing this hymn I seem to be paddling a little leaf-shaped canoe against the swift current of a river, and I am brought back to the world of my father's past. When I recall his whole life, a life abundant in truth, beauty, and goodness, my heart is filled with irresistible passion and charming inspiration. Like waves on a rough sea, this inner inspiration lashes me and murmurs in my soul: For your great father, the most valuable, influential, and respected person in your life, you must tell people of today about his life, which was an unending battle against difficulties and social vices, a lonely and courageous struggle through darkness. In this world, so filled with vices and dominated by so many selfish people with a crazy lust for fame, there is a wide spiritual distance between human hearts, and a portrait of your father's life will shine in sharp contrast to the predominating ugliness like a pure white lily or a charming summer lotus flower standing alone in a muddy pond. The beauty and purity of his personality may help to keep alive people's enthusiasm for pursuing a beautiful and meaningful life.

His life experiences as a dutiful son, as a faithful husband, as a gracious and influential father, as a great teacher, and above all as a shining Christian make his example one worthy of continual sharing with the strangers of this world. For he has left behind imperishably beautiful traces in human hearts, and he reminds me of the unfinished and the touching chimes of the bell of vigilance.

A PURE LILY IN
THE WILDERNESS

2

THE BIRTH OF MY FATHER, THE REVEREND Li Yuan Mo, was as lacking in news worthiness as the new budding of a lily in the wilderness. It was apparently of no importance to the human eye, yet throughout his life as in that of others, God visualizes for us His intelligent and purposeful plan for each human being, His peerless loving care for each of His earthly children. My father's birth reflects the great mystery of our Almighty Creator of the Universe.

Born in a small and rather secluded village named Kou-Dien, in Hanyang, Hupei Province, in the Yangtze River valley, in the year of 1871, he was the third son of a typically conservative and honest farmer. My grandparents believed in Buddhism. As they had only a few acres to till, the yield was not sufficient to maintain my grandfather's big family, which consisted of a wife, three sons, two daughters-in-law, and his mother, who was my great-grandmother. My grandparents had to resort to tailoring and spinning as side occupations in order to earn enough to cover family expenditures. My father once told us that he helped to look after the cows and did the minor chores on the farm. Two older brothers helped with the farming. From the time he was born, he lived the hard, struggling life of a farmer.

Toiling daily in the rice fields, he was impressed with the many admirable facets of God's creation through intimate contacts with the natural beauty of His world. He observed the consistent order of the heavenly bodies, the implications of eternity of the sun and the moon, the living process of a seed developing into a bushy plant, the tender branch budding into fragrant flower, the beauty of the trees, the melodious singing of the little birds that nest in them, enchanting human ears, the white clouds wandering through the blue sky, the morning dew on the thirsty grass and flowers, the slow-moving cows as they served mankind, the glittering waves of the river in the sunlight, the folds of the hills beyond the rice fields, blanketed with jade-green plants—all these beautiful facets of Nature were engraved in the little curious soul of my father when he was young. He began to wonder about the source of these childhood impressions.

He was a brilliant, industrious and dutiful son, and was always willing to help others. Hence, he was the pet of his parents. At the age of five, he lost his mother. Her death was a terrific blow to his tender heart. The loss of a mother's love leaves a spiritual emptiness that can never be compensated for or filled by any substitute.

After the death of my grandmother, my father told me that he had tried hard to be the comforter to his lonely father. He endeavored to be more dutiful. Following his older brothers, he farmed in the field, looked after the cows, and helped to do the housework that his mother used to do. He was born with a loving heart that was considerate when others were involved.

A little before he was seven years old, my father was sent to a private village school called She-Su, to receive his primary education. It was an old-fashioned one-room school with meager equipment, and an old stern-faced teacher with a long whip to enforce obedience. The Four Books, the Five Classics, and handwriting were the basic curriculum. My father was held to be the most brilliant and assiduous boy among all the sons of the villagers. He had such a good memory that he could recite all classical passages as fluently as running water flows; even more, he could recite them in reverse order. He always won first place in examinations. Thus, he was highly valued and recognized by the whole village. My grandfather loved him so dearly he liked to dream that someday in the future the boy would become a great scholar (*Shiu-Tsai*, which means a chosen and talented intellectual), and eventually serve in the Central Government as a prominent official through competitive examination.

It was the ambition of all Chinese parents in the early days to train their sons to be scholars, because only those with excellent scholarship could become high government officials. My grandfather did not want his son to follow in his own footsteps, and remain a hard-working farmer, holding a plow with one hand and trailing a cow with the other. But how could a humble farmer's son become a great man, whose anticipated achievements could bring glory to his family, his ancestors, and his place of origin? Such a goal seemed as unreachable as a castle in the air! Within my grandfather's heart there was a bitter conflict between idealism and reality!

Consider the lilies. They were born in the wilderness in seeming neglect, and yes, there is often the invisible Creator who cares for such out-of-the-way plants in silence. My father's destiny was shepherded by the same Creator!

While my father was studying in the village school, he never failed to work on the farm during his other hours. He said he often carried farm products such as rice, potatoes, or vegetables on his frail shoulders to market in the neighborhood towns and sold them out at retail. While he plowed the fields under the blazing summer sun or carried heavy loads of farm products attached to a bamboo rod in wintry weather, he never forgot to recite the classical assignments that his teacher had taught him. My grandfather loved him because of his unusual assiduity, his sense of responsibility, and his unceasing search for knowledge. But, when my grandfather reflected upon his meager income and realized the handicap it was to further his son's education, he was both ashamed and worried.

A miracle was wrought in the life of my father. Christianity had spread through the coastal cities of China in the beginning of the nineteenth century. The West came into contact with the East through Christianity. Yellow-haired and blue-eyed American missionaries began to erect schools in different cities. They wished to benefit worthy and underprivileged youngsters with free Christian education. In 1880 free Christian schools were also erected in Wuchang, the capital of Hupei Province in the Yangtze River valley by pioneer American missionaries of the Episcopal Church, specifically the American Church Mission. My grandfather was thrilled with joy when this news was conveyed to his ears. Through the recommendations of several influential village leaders, my father was admitted to one of these Christian schools. My father said that he was loved by the American missionary at first sight, and left the impression with them of a pleasant and bright boy. His entrance at the gate of the Christian school was the prelude to a new and meaningful life. It was a hard but an abundant life, a significantly great and fabulous call from Heaven. At that time, my father was seventeen years of age.

Carrying his simple bedding and a wooden trunk, he entered on a new path of life with optimistic enthusiasm and a genuine admiration for knowledge. He viewed this opportunity as if he had found Solomon's mines! He treasured it and made the best use of it with unfailing effort.

In only half a year, he had made remarkable intellectual progress. He had an excellent grasp of his schoolwork and developed real insight into all branches of knowledge. When he was a young boy, most of his learning were merely swallowed mentally but undigested. Now he had a really enlightened approach and a keen interest in what he was learning. Within a year's time, his progress was marvelously rapid.

The passing of time has brought about better mutual understanding among individuals in different races. Blue eyes and yellow hair, black eyes and black hair—these are only superficial differences between human races. As to intelligence, thought process, and the response to external stimuli, there are no significant differences between races any more than there are between individuals. As time went by, my father impressed his teachers as being a promising youth. His performance assured them of his many-sided excellences, for literary talent, intelligence, persistence, determined will power, a sense of responsibility, a sense of righteousness, and a blending of such invaluable qualities as integrity and social-mindedness—all these were deeply rooted in the character of the humble Chinese farmer's son. The American missionaries congratulated themselves on their choice of this worthy boy. They believed that poverty should not bury human talents and thus bar human progress. My father's case strengthened their conviction that every human being has been endowed with a special gift in accordance with God's purpose. Poverty should not be a shame to any worthy youth. Christian education should search out such worthy abilities and talents and render them serviceable to the common good of mankind. My father's case provided them with realistic proof of their assumption and reinforced their optimistic outlook on future educational and religious work in China.

As the wheel of time rotated, my father attained not only intellectual growth, but developed deeply in his soul a Christian outlook on life through the influence of the sacrificial love and sympathy of his American missionary teachers.

At the age of eighteen, he went back to see his father during the summer vacation. He brought a string of copper coins. (old Chinese currency was made of copper with a hole in the center.) My father said that he had saved the coins from his monthly allowance. He gave them to his dear father as a present. My grandfather was overwhelmed and deeply touched by his son's filial piety and his thriftiness.

As all normal parents are happy to see their beloved children after an absence, so was my grandfather at the return of his son from a distant place, especially as he came back with scholastic honors. But one thing marred this moment of exceeding delight and affectionate reunion. Being a pious devotee to Buddhism, my grandfather ordered my father to kneel down before the Buddha and the portraits of his ancestors in the living room. This was a traditional courtesy by which one expressed one's respect and heartfelt gratitude for the blessings given by Buddha and one's ancestors. My grandfather was naturally thankful for the glorious return and for the magnificent educational opportunity given to his son by his god.

"No, dear father, I cannot kneel down before a false god and adore him. Will you please forgive me?"

This rebellious response both shocked and irritated the conservative and superstitious father.

"What! These foreigners have poisoned my beloved son's mind with their bewitching foreign ghost religion (*Yang Chiao*)! Should I continue to allow him to study in their school, he will no longer even respect his hard-working father on the farm," he shouted. "If he believes in a foreign religion and does not worship the Buddha or respect his ancestors, he will turn out to be a dangerous and revolutionary element in my family. He could ruin the whole village." My grandfather was overcome by mingled anger, fear, and disappointment.

After this revolutionary behavior, the rural family that usually lived in simple tranquility and harmonious contentment became a distressed place, where often was heard the scolding voice of an angry father directed toward the misunderstood son.

"If one has a son who believes and 'eats' the poisoned imported religion until it is in his mind and blood, what is any good, after all," sighed the father of my father with heart-struck melancholy. My grandfather was so upset and frustrated that he could hardly refrain from anticipating all sorts of horrible consequences that a Christian education would eventually bring into his son's mind and heart.

His attitude toward his son fluctuated from fearlessness to self-contradiction, from self-contradiction to indignation, from indignation to hate. He finally determined to stop my father from attending any longer the free Christian school at Wuchang.

Born and nurtured as a dutiful and obedient son, my father accepted his father's fear, indignation and stubbornness with great calmness and quiet patience. The more he sensed his father's indignation, the greater his problem became. There was created in his lonely heart a bitter conflict between affection and reason, between right against wrong. He had to choose between truth and falsehood. My father underwent a crucial experience of inner spiritual affliction.

One can picture his mental state at this period. He was like a small, lonely leaf-like boat tossed on a rough boundless sea. He felt the presence of danger, solitude, and helplessness at this desperate moment of his life. Although under painful emotional stress, he was nevertheless daring in spirit.

Father told me that during this period of unhappy confinement at home, he did not express any outward sign of resentment. He passed through the spiritual struggle with uncomplaining heroism. In lieu of self-pity, he sublimated his personal difficulties by positive and constructive means. He tried to win his father's heart and to comfort him with patience and greater filial piety. He willingly helped to do all kinds of humble work in the house and in the fields.

Torn by hatred and suspicion, my old grandfather really thought that his son's heart had been poisoned by what he called the "foreign devil's religion," and imposed on my father the toughest and most unpleasant tasks on the farm.

On one autumn morning, he commanded my father to carry eighty catties (about one hundred pounds) of grain to a market about forty li (thirteen and one half miles) away from the village. My father obeyed without feeling any shame as many Chinese intellectuals might have felt at this lowly task. Although my father had doubts that his frail body could bear such a heavy load to so distant a place on foot, yet he tried. He labored along, resting every five li. From early morning till noon, he had walked only two thirds of the way. On the last ten li he was desperately exhausted. His shoulders were so sore and feet so tired that he could barely move forward. During this critical experience he realized the smallness of human strength. He felt the pressing need of a superhuman and divine power to help him in his desperation; he needed greater faith and patience. My father said that he knelt down beside the lonesome road and prayed to God to strengthen his weak shoulders, to reinforce him with added courage, so that he could accomplish what his father had entrusted him to do and make him happy. He prayed thus: "O my heavenly Father have mercy upon me by giving me a chance to manifest my whole-hearted filial piety to my father. Please give me new strength for my frail body; give me courage to lift this heavy load again; help me finish this hard journey so that my father shall regain his lost confidence in me and be pleased in what I have done for him!"

God answered his prayer. He heard a voice say: "Lift up, lift up again the heavy burden bravely. I shall grant you strength to walk the rest of the journey!" Like a gentle breeze blowing over him, my father felt the presence of the Holy Spirit. His strength and courage were reinforced, and he was enabled to complete the journey. He reached the market. He sold all the grain. When he came back at twilight of that day, he handed his father the money. His father was moved to tears by the victorious smile radiating from his son's exhausted soul!

My grandfather was a hard-working, industrious, and thrifty farmer. He embodied the noble Chinese virtues: simplicity and integrity. He was a widower most of his life, a man charged with the double responsibility of being both a provider and a mother. He was virtuous and highly appreciated by his fellow villagers. My father pitied his parent's solitude. Although he was an intellectual who had had scholastic training, particularly a Western education, he was not at all arrogant or sophisticated as many intellectuals are.

Education had bred in him a deeper sense of sympathy and understanding of human feelings and misery. When he saw his old father, his back bent, toiling strenuously in the fields, or with busy fingers sewing in the dim light of the vegetable-oil lamp, trying to earn a livelihood for his loved ones, pity seized him and emotion brought a lump to his throat. Education to him meant not only intellectual development but deeper insight into human desires and problems. He was not proud of his story for his worldly knowledge, rather he became more humble as his scholarship widened. A Chinese proverb says: "To be boastful with knowledge invites destruction; a humble attitude brings greater benefits." My father believed this. The higher he climbed on the intellectual ladder, the greater understanding of the human nature he became. He helped his father with the cooking on the clay kitchen stove; he chopped wood for fuel; he tended the pigs and chickens and did all kinds of menial work. He realized that to be a dutiful son and to help the poor were ways of manifesting the highest form of human virtue.

Enduring hardships without complaint, my father gradually convinced his own dear father of his love and affection. His father said: "I have been mistaken and prejudiced. At first, I took for granted that to believe in the foreign devil's religion and to read its books would poison my son's heart. But, I found out that the reverse was true. My son is not proud at all; actually, he is more humble and considerate. Christian education has done him more good than harm. His behavior and character have become unbelievably polished and decent."

My grandfather finally became convinced of the beneficial effects of Western education through the inspiring conduct of his son during the young man's three months' imprisonment at home. From that time on, his attitude changed, and he again became loving and kind as he had been before. His fears and animosity melted away in the sunny behavior of his son. Time changes all things!

The school authorities wrote to my father asking him to return. Faced with a dilemma compounded by fear and love, my grandfather had to make a decision. While he feared his beloved son might be seduced into pride and vanity by Western civilization, his love and sympathy for the young man and his knowledge that his frail health made him unsuitable for farming as a career warred within him. Finally, his love for his son won out. He granted permission to his son to go to school again. It was a brave decision for an old-fashioned farmer to make in the nineteenth century.

My father's filial devotion overcame the ignorant stubbornness of his Buddhist father. But it took many more years to convert his father to Christianity. Time and patience helped my father to inspire others, including his immediate family and his friends, to believe in the God he believed.

My father was like a pure and attractive lily whose beauty and fragrance were shared by the entire field. Many a lonely lily in a remote field is seemingly neglected by human eyes; it is in constant danger of being trodden into the ground by heedless animals. Yet, there is always an omnipotent, omniscient, and omnipresent Creator watching over it and encouraging its growth until it becomes unequaled and unexcelled among its kind.

THE MAGNIFICENT TURNING POINT

3

MY FATHER LEFT HIS HOME AND HIS DEAR FATHER and the brothers to further his education at the Christian school in Wuchang, thirty-five miles away. He left with a heart filled with spiritual conviction. His departure was the starting point of a crusade against ungodliness and social evils that played a major part in his life's journey. Like a detached warrior on a confusing battlefield, he had to devise his own strategy and fight his battles alone. Every obstacle was a new challenge to him.

After my father's departure, his own father's heart contained a conflict of emotions: a struggle between Western and Eastern ideals; between pagan and Christian beliefs; between truth and prejudice.

Now that my father had again an opportunity for further education, he pursued his studies relentlessly. Within two years, he showed the result of his perseverance, having made remarkable progress in all his academic studies and in understanding Chinese classics in light of Western culture. His outlook on life changed as his natural talents were revealed and reorientated. He was highly regarded and profoundly admired by his teachers.

At the age of nineteen, he made an important decision. He felt a divine call from within. In the world around him he felt himself to be a piece of seaweed floating on a boundless sea. He was very much concerned about his sinful soul and the souls of many others of his time. My father told me that his determination to be a minister came as a spontaneous urge from his inner soul, not as a pressure from without. It was an irresistible demand.

When he observed the consistent order of the universe, its vastness, and its peerless beauty, he said, repeating Psalm 19, verses 1–3: *"The heavens declare the glory of God; and the firmament showeth his handiwork. Day unto day uttereth speech, and night unto night showeth knowledge. There is no speech nor language, where their voice is not heard."*

He realized that there is nothing so inspiring as to follow God the Creator—the omnipotent, omnipresent, and omniscient Master—and to spread His truth and wisdom among the needy, the poor, the selfish, and the miserable. There is no nobler career in life than to guide people to walk in the path of truth, beauty, and righteousness. So he determined to devote his life to God, and walked humbly with Him.

He had anticipated his father's opposition to his choice. However, he could not resist this divine call from within. He decided that, despite his love for his father, he would be a preacher of God's teachings. So he entered the School of Theology at Boone University, in Wuchang, capital of Hupei Province. This later became a well-known Episcopal university in Central China. In 1894, at the age of twenty-three, my father became a professed clergyman, and started his ministry in the diocese of Hupei Province.

The American bishops, during this pioneer period, first recognized the fitness of my father's personality for such a dignified profession. During his theological training, Bishop Soo and Bishop Kou discovered that he had wisdom, courage, determination, and broad vision. He had great creative talent, and lofty ideals. In his early years, my father said, he was appointed to write and translate the church hymns of the Episcopal Church from English into Chinese, under the direction of the presiding bishop of Hupei Diocese. Nearly all the hymns of the Episcopal Church were translated by my father at that time. Besides, he wrote many of his own, when his children were very small. Number 352 in the *Universal Hymn Book* is one of his original hymns. I did not know this until 1954, when I happened to buy a copy of the *Universal Hymn Book* in a bookstore in Hong Kong. I was deeply inspired by the discovery; that is why, at the beginning of this memoir, I have used it as a kind of prelude to set the tone for what comes after.

My father's spiritual enlightenment and biblical insight did not come to him by chance, but by thorough and persistent search, unfailing assiduity, and daily absorption of the spiritual nutrients and vitality in God's Holy Book. He not only preached to others, but every day of his life he built up his spiritual conviction and maintained his moral health by drawing on the dynamic power of God from the Bible.

He lived very close to God, for he was confident that, in this troubled and perplexing world, there is nothing more perfect and happier than to communicate with God in solitude and in intimate privacy. My father thought of prayer as a triple procedure: ask, seek, and knock. Throughout his whole life, he asked in faith, sought diligently, and knocked at God's door sincerely and persistently. When I was very small, I remembered that right after the dawn of each day, after the cock crowed his first awakening song in our backyard, it was always followed by my father's devotional prayer, spoken alone and aloud. Every day of his life, he never failed to polish and beautify his inner self by intimate communication with the Lord, and he lived according to His precepts and His will. From the age of twenty-three to his death at age eighty-one, he devoted more than a half century of his time to the service of God.

My father's life was creative and productive, not a consuming one, it was filled with bitter, heart-stricken episodes, but hardly one filled with gaiety. But as St. Paul says: "But I labored more abundantly than they all." He labored with devout willingness and integrity; he endeavored to be a good shepherd under Jesus Christ.

The totality of his greatness consists of many tiny drops and forgotten deeds of kindness and goodness. An anonymous hero, he dedicated himself to the worthy and needful cause that he enthusiastically and relentlessly pursued. The whole picture of his life, I dare declare on my conscience, is the best portrait possible of a man with a magnificent and charming inwardness.

My father's decision, at nineteen, was an important turning point in his destiny as well as in the destiny of rising generations. It shows how God sometimes unexpectedly summons us to new responsibilities. Like Peter and Andrew, who received the divine challenge as they went about their familiar task as fisherman, my father surprised his old-fashioned father, and his family too, in the midst of their routine of farming life. God came into his life and he was called to a new kind of loyalty and devotion. It was a new orientation, resulting from an unexpected combination of circumstances.

A LONELY SOWER

4

TIME CLARIFIES IMPRESSIONS OF PEOPLE WE HAVE known a long time. My father is implanted in the minds of his bishops and senior church ministers as a man of trustworthy character and a charming spiritual outpouring. Steeped in both Chinese classical teaching and Western Christian education, he chose the best from each cultural heritage and blended them into a beautiful functional harmony. Confucius's wise teaching formed the background of my father's moral philosophy. Sincerity is the absolute essential, according to Confucius, but he was also inconsistent upon ability. Confucius maintained that society was an ordinance of Heaven made up of five relationships, namely, ruler and subject, father and son, elder brother and young brother, husband and wife, friend and friend. Rule should by righteousness and benevolence on the part of the first four; submission to rule should be marked by righteousness and sincerity. Between friends, the mutual promotion of virtue should be the guiding principle. This was the great spiritual ideal my father learned prior to his Christian education. This spirit, too, has shaped the moral life of the Chinese people. Confucius is the cornerstone of Chinese civilization and of China's ethical standards. Christian teaching had much in common with Confucius's ideology. It was auxiliary rather than contradictory in the development of my father's moral character.

Both in his work and in his life, my father manifested all the exquisite qualities of his inner self. Like a rose, his fragrance emerged from his character to those who had contacts with him. My father often held that "in this sorry world, more and more good people, people with Christian faith and courage, are needed to sustain the peace and welfare of mankind." He held to this conviction as he traveled the zigzag path of his life journey.

He had a soft yet zealous heart, a creative and active mind, a persistent vitality, a fearless spirit, and a soul faithful to God. From his twenty-third year, he was entrusted with more and more difficult tasks. He was assigned to seek uncultivated lands in which to erect God's houses. He trampled through barren fields and jungles in wildernesses, often alone. His mission was to turn the barren lands into green pastures and livable farms. Inspired by the sunshine of each morning, he sought to bring his preaching to every societal dark spot. It was a tough task, and one that required special human qualities.

But there was a force pushing him to work fearlessly and confidently. The Bible says: *"And the Lord said, If ye had faith as a grain of mustard seed, ye might say unto this sycamine tree, Be thou plucked up by the root, and be thou planted in the sea; and it should obey you"* (Luke 17:6). He thought on this; he believed in it; and he used it in his struggle. To turn barren fields into green pastures; to turn darkness into light; to convert ignorance into enlightenment; to change selfishness into self-sacrifice; to turn hatred into benevolence; to change sadness into gaiety; human segregation to integration; antagonism to agreement— these are the hardest problems in the world. But my father's life constitutes a complete answer book to all these intricate perplexing and difficult problems.

Although Christianity was introduced into China sometime in the Tang Dynasty (618–906), it had a long struggle before it gained popularity among Chinese people. Nestorian Christianity had survived at the border of China since the Tang dynasty and reappeared again in the Yuan dynasty (1260–1368). In this last period, Europeans made their way to China for the first time. The first missionary to reach China was the Franciscan Giovanni De Monte Corvino, who arrived in 1294 at Cambaluc, and after three decades or more had built up a Christian community of several thousand. Following him came a number of other missionaries, notably Giovanna De Marignolli. After the collapse of Mongol rule, the trade routes became unsafe and antiforeign reaction set in. Europeans, both merchants and missionaries, disappeared from China, and the Catholic Nestorian communities passed out of existence.

Until the Manchus, Catholic missionaries continued to come, because Emperor K'ang Hsi had issued an edict of religious toleration. For a number of years the church prospered greatly. Missionaries and Christian communities were found in all provinces, and by 1700 the Catholics in the empire probably numbered more than three hundred thousand. Then came a series of reverses. A prolonged controversy arose over what Chinese term should be used for "God," and what attitude should be taken by Christians toward certain Chinese rites, among them the honor paid to ancestors and Confucius. The cultural conflicts resulted in religious indifference, so that by 1800 Catholics in China had dropped to about two hundred thousand. Between 1600–1800, however, Catholic missionaries had helped to acquaint China with European science and religion, and by their writings had spread in Europe a knowledge of Chinese culture.

The industrial revolution of the nineteenth century in England inaugurated a period of renewed expansion of occidental influence. After the opium war with Britain, which resulted in the Nanking Treaty, there followed another foreign war with Britain, which resulted in the Tientsin Treaty. One of the treaties sanctioned Christian missionaries and Christians, both foreign and Chinese, were guaranteed freedom in the practice of their faith. From that time on, Christian missionaries, both Roman Catholic and Protestants, rapidly increased in number. And the influence of Christianity played a considerably significant part in modernizing China, and in promoting the social, educational, and ethical progress of the Chinese people.

For most of my father's missionary life, he was engaged in the pioneer work of planting churches and establishing Christian communities in barren places. But his most significant and difficult task was to fill these new churches with devoted lovers of God. At the close of the nineteenth century, when my father began to shoulder this chosen responsibility, he encountered mounting difficulties. Missionaries, at that time, had to deal with Chinese who had strong cultural pride and powerfully resisted change. They had to accept the fact that Chinese people had a long history of devotion to the teachings of Confucius, and those of other ethical systems: mainly Buddhism and Taoism. Missionaries had to preach to an overwhelmingly agricultural people, who, because of China's geographical position, were self-contained, conservative-minded, and superstitious. So, to do missionary work, to form churches here and there in towns and in rural districts, was a tremendous challenge. My father realized that to convince and guide the people, rural and predominately illiterate, or to urge proud scholars to step humbly into these new churches, was no easier than for the camel to go through the eye of a needle. It was as speculative as to result as Columbus's search for a new land of promise.

Who were most suitable and reliable as cultivators? This question had to be answered before any pioneering was begun. Much of the responsibility rested on the shoulders of my father during that pioneer period.

Under the burning sun of summer, goaded by the pricking wind of winter, he labored incessantly. Wearing a pair of home-made cloth shoes (usually made by my mother) and a simple cotton Chinese gown, he walked miles and miles every day, climbing high mountains, crossing rivers on a small wooden *sampan*, passing through lonesome graveyards, he searched for a suitable land for God's lost sheep. He supervised humble laborers who were set to dispose of loads and loads of corpses and human bones, to shear off the thorny grass in the wilderness; to level the rough ground and all the tasks necessary for foundation work. Calmly and competently, he contemplated the engineering plan of each church. He supervised the tasks daily till each building plan had become a church for solemn worship. He made others forget the melancholy, barren land that once evoked the fear of death as one passed by, for out of the newly built church issued cheerful and glorious singing, dispelling loneliness, and the church school and campus, occupied by lively children, were in sharp contrast to the former emptiness. These changes were made possible by the dynamic, forceful, unfailing persistence and sacrificial spirit of God's cultivators, who attained them by spending many lonesome years and months in the work.

My father's footsteps were printed on the lands along the Yangtze River valley, from Hupei, the upper branch of the Yangtze down to Kiangsi and Anhui provinces (see map). He helped to establish churches in several large cities, namely, Kiuchiang, King Tei Cheng, Anking, and Wuhu, as well as in their surrounding small towns and districts. He sowed in every reachable, unbelieving land to cultivate Christian gardens. He changed the barren lands into green pastures. He loved to plant trees. Wherever he founded churches and schools, he plowed the earth and sowed the seeds himself. He watered the ground himself and was happy when his seeds grew roots and became tall and lovely trees. The trees planted shelters for his church members and their children. They serve to recall many priceless memories.

To build the highway toward God's Kingdom, my father kept busy in his customary, self-forgetting way. He never budgeted for his future welfare and personal prosperity. When he saw that the church foundation had been laid and the plants and the flowers were with a victorious smile! He let other men of God continue what he had started. Full of spiritual strength and conviction, he awaited God's next call. Like a farmer, he enjoyed this eternal recurrence of cultivation and growth of God's work. His life was a continuous searching, but he could not sit still and enjoy the harvest reaped by others. Throughout his life, he lived in meager simplicity—coarse cotton clothing and simple meals. He was thrifty for himself but generous to others. He made no demand on vanity and fame. His philosophy of life was to live life abundantly and to help others by his mere existence.

He was renowned for his fidelity and devout loyalty. "Your father is a number one minister," commented one of my father's American friends, James Pott, who had served as the principal of St. Paul's Boys' School in Anking, in Anhui Diocese. My father never craved for power or material gain. He taught his children that a person's honesty was best testified to in the handling of other people's property. That was one of his famous proverbs. His self-reliance stemmed from his honesty. He hated to see sinful desires in the human heart to increase material wealth by covetous behavior. He was regarded as a striking example of a completely honest man by all those who worked with him. The Chinese philosophy holds that "he who renounces fame has no sorrow," and also, "contentment brings joy to a man even though he is in poverty." These sayings typify my father's moral character exactly.

Traveling unfailingly, he wanted to see churches opened everywhere. He went on round after round of begging visits to strangers. He wanted to find God's lost sheep and people with troubled souls. He loved and valued every member, poor or rich. He continuously recruited new members here and there. He helped prevent them from sinking into sin and vice. He found preaching a great joy, a glorious privilege, as did Paul. He concentrated mind, heart, and body in a struggle to awaken unbelievers, for the expansion of the Christian ministry in China.

Spiritual growth or moral reconstruction has proved to be more difficult and time-consuming than material changes in a nation's history. To instill Christian faith in the minds of the Chinese people proved an even harder task!

While constructing the highway for God, my father realized that the world depressingly gloomy, filled with widespread suffering and evil. He was aware that he was born to an age of a spiritual decadence in mankind. Christ-hating savages, ugly-souled creatures with a zealous and feverish greed for worldly gain and of power, had driven the whole of mankind to a insatiable hunger for lasting peace. He realized that materialism could not alone save the world. Spiritual reform and mobilization are needed to bring human hearts into a harmonious relationship. The divine blessing of the Christian ideology of brotherhood and benevolence had to be instilled into human souls. It alone was the clue to the solution of human misery.

The more that society is darkened by evil-doers, the more explicitly it implied to my father that there were innumerable souls waiting for spiritual revival and salvation. He felt that the pressure of his burden became heavier and heavier. He faced the mounting challenges of Christian responsibilities lying ahead of him.

His preaching career was most rough and exhausting. He had met almost unsurmountable difficulties—sarcasm, spite, condemnation, and the cursing antagonism of ignorant, proud, and self-righteous people. Despite these obstacles and spiritual setbacks, he kept on working optimistically through darkness, for he relied on God for courage, strength, and vitality to carry on this great mission. He sought in every corner of the community to make contacts with people of all sorts and classes, begging their recognition of God. He had to suffer many humiliations to strive forward, because he wanted to serve as a beacon light to those who had been sinking into complete darkness in more ways than one. This meant to him a prodigious amount of continuous and strenuous seeking.

But he brought many of God's lost sheep among the Chinese people into the fold, and guided them to knock upon the "narrow gate" of God's house! He conquered their fear, hatred, antagonism, stupidity, and pride. He finally tamed their wildness and greed for worldly things and built up a Christian concern for life. How did he win disciples for God?

There are three major reasons that account for his success in recruiting so many Christian believers.

First, his sympathetic infiltration into human hearts. He illustrated his faith by his own life. Throughout his whole life, he never failed to do a good deed that would help a needy person. He grasped every visible chance to apply Christian principles to life. In addition to preaching to ignorant people to do good and to love their neighbors, he actually loved them individually. My father cared for them when they were sick, or in need of any material help that he or the church could give. He visited every member of his church regularly, and helped whoever was in desperate circumstances. As a daughter, I praise him as a great man of God, whose greatness was built up by many small things, by innumerable tiny kind and affectionate deeds here and there. He held that God's plan was that every human being had a right to live and hence should live a purposeful life according to God's will! He won the hearts of people through virtuous and inspiriting actions. In his preaching, he entered sympathetically into the heart of each member. He always studied, scrutinizing closely, people's needs and problems, spiritual physical or material. He was a great Christian, in action.

Second, he undertook constant and persistent guidance of the spiritual life of the members. He taught every stranger he met to know God and understand His teaching by constant and patient guidance. Every day he visited his members to teach them how to pray. To teach illiterates God's precepts and how to pray is not an easy task. Yet, my father had such a persistent patience that he tried to teach every stranger he met how to communicate with God in a personal way.

For instance, an old country woman of eighty lived deep in a backward village in Tai-Hu, in Anking, Anhui. She was helpless and lonely, and her only income was derived from raising a few pigs. My father discovered her while doing evangelistic work in that area, in 1915. He went to see her, and comforted her by telling her that there is a God who is our heavenly father in Heaven. My father said that if she prayed to Him, He would surely look after her and make her happy. This sounded like complete nonsense—an unbelievable fairy tale—to the old, illiterate woman, whose mind has been open only to Buddhism. She responded stubbornly: "I am illiterate; I don't know how to pray!" My father asked her if she remembered, when she was small, asking help and favors from her parents. That reminded the old woman. She seemed to get the secret of how to communicate with God. My father came to visit the old woman frequently. Whenever he went to her house, the question "Have you prayed?" was asked.

The old lady always answered with a smile: "Yes, Pastor, I prayed."

"How did you pray?" my father would ask.

The old lady would answer, "O merciful God, please kindly look after my pigs, my only hope of existence, and let them grow healthy and fat quickly so I can sell them at a good price." That was her prayer.

My father would nod. "That is the way you talk to God." He was happy because the old woman began to rely on God as her guide for life. The smiles that radiated from her old, wrinkled face assured him that she recognized her Heavenly Father.

Third, his constant daily absorption of spiritual nutrition from the Holy Bible. He not only preached to others; every day of his life he built up his spiritual maturity by deriving dynamic power for a Christian life and happiness from the Bible. He lived according to His precepts and walked humbly with Him. Every evening, after supper, there was evening prayer in our family; even the servants were urged to attend. Father read Scripture to us and explained it. Often, he asked us what he had been talking about in order to measure our concentration and daily attainment during the family service. He thought that a clergyman should first assure himself, as a faithful Christian, that every member of his family, his relatives, and the next generations should endeavor to be shining Christian examples.

The more he sought, the more he discovered the need for seeking. He never wanted to stop, but to keep on extending his ministry to more and other directions. He sought through every layer of society, and every traceable corner of human habitation in his time. He grasped every opportunity to preach, big or small. He believed that spiritual reformation is the root of all social betterment, moral uplift the source of human progress. The progress of human civilization should be founded on integrity and righteousness. Raising of ethical standards should be the first fundamental task to be stressed in any age and in any nation. That is why he was so ambitiously solemn, insistently persistent, practical and humble in his dedication to the gigantic task of guiding people to explore the truth—the only truth—and hope that control the destiny of mankind.

A PRODIGIOUS
SEARCHING

5

MY FATHER'S EVER-INCREASING DESIRE TO HELP others kept him constantly active. He wanted everyone to live an abundant and useful life.

As he observed the many facets of human society, he discovered that millions of people were spiritually lonesome and materially desperate. Poverty went hand in hand with ignorance. Poverty was a cruel enemy to the sick, whose lives were shortened through inability to pay for medical care; ambitious and worthy people were humiliated because of poverty; so-called righteous people snobbishly avoided the poor as their social inferiors.

He saw that poverty checked human progress and buried millions of talents. He denounced the social habit of judging a person's worthiness by his material wealth. The more a person has, the higher he is on the social ladder. The wealthiest perch on the top rung of the social ladder. He denounced as unfair the evaluation of social value on the basis of material possessions. The practice, he said, stimulates greed, selfishness, envy, and hatred. It blinds people to what is really worthwhile in life. He contended that human worth and value should be determined by what one contributes to the common good of all.

He firmly believed that Christian teaching should endeavor to broaden human vision and alter the prevailing method of weighing human worth, Christian concern for others should act to emancipate the poor from spiritual torture and social discrimination. Christianity is functional and should help heavily laden and contrite hearts to be optimistic, to look forward with hope, and to build self-assurance and dignity.

My father said that when he felt the sunshine, which shone alike on the good and wicked, the rich and the poor, the happy and the sad, he derived great inspiration from it and a fabulous revelation of God's immeasurable love for all mankind. This simple yet mysterious natural phenomenon was symbolic of God's generous affection.

My father encouraged talent in needy youngsters while he was preaching the gospel. He was more than a preacher of God's truth; he was a man of Christian action. He did

God's will by following Jesus Christ's example to enter into the daily life of the people with genuine sincerity and loving kindness. Like the freshening power of morning dew, he gladdened many contrite hearts. He changed desert-dry minds into hopeful oases. His moral support and affection toward the poor and the needy were a turning point in their lives and brought light and hope to their desperate souls. Here are some stories of his experiences.

LINTER TSENG'S STORY

Linter was an orphan who had had no one to care for him since he was six years old but an old grandmother. The grandmother was over sixty. She and Linter lived in a shabby hut on a lonely hill near a village in Anhui Province. Her only means of livelihood was gathering dead branches for firewood and planting vegetables, when her frail health would permit. Linter lived only for the present, for every tomorrow loomed uncertain and vague. He and his grandmother were virtually destitute.

Lither was a bright boy and made a nice appearance. He was a treasure to his grandmother, a priceless pearl.

My father heard about Linter and encouraged him to enter the church school of which he was principal. He soon discovered that Linter was a talented child, with superior intelligence and fine linguistic ability. He kept his eye on him. The child became close to my father's tender heart, and he determined to do everything he could to give this young life purposeful direction.

As time went on, Linter proved himself a worthy boy, deserving both the assistance of the church and of my father. However, his problem was not simply the need of material help; there was also to be overcome his conservative grandmother's resistance to any help that came from the Christian church.

Linter's grandmother was like most Chinese villagers, stubborn and resenting change; especially she was anti-Christian. But my father was firm. He had made up his mind to educate this youngster and convert him to Christianity, for he has glimpsed the hidden worth and the unlimited potentialities God had given Linter.

My father told me that he made constant visits to the old lady on the lonely hill, which took him an hour to climb the steep path. He tried every way to persuade her. He assured her that the church was so interested in her grandson that it would help him to get the best education possible without any financial obligation.

The old lady, fearing separation from her beloved grandson, became antagonistic and refused to believe my father's kind intention.

"There is no such thing as a kindhearted person in this world!" she insisted. "No one will support my grandson for nothing, giving him food, room, clothing, tuition, and all sorts of other things without a cent in return. Your words are tempting and flowery, but I can see the underlying plan!" The old lady twisted the truth and flatly refused my father's offer. She feared the church might kidnap her brilliant grandson and take him to a foreign country. My father was not irritated by her rejection. Instead, he left her with a courteous smile. But he decided to visit her again and persist in his attempt to help Linter.

He came more and more frequently. Did these visits with the old lady promote good will and end in mutual agreement? No! The more my father went to see her, the firmer she was in misinterpreting his motives. Her anger was intensified, and her antagonism arose, whenever she saw my father climbing up the hill toward her. She was fiercely offended, in fact. She even tried to hide her grandson.

Still my father persisted; he must win Linter for God. He made the trip over and over again. Once, the old lady became so wrathful that she cursed him, shouting, "If you dare to come here again, I will break your leg!"

My father remained calm. He responded with a smile, "I am responsible to my God. I love Linter, so I come to visit you. Why do you get so angry? Perhaps, today you are tired from gathering wood and planting vegetables and your fatigue has made you emotionally irritable. I think I will leave you in peace, today, and come to see you again."

For the sake of this precious young life, this promising child, my father felt that anything was bearable, if at last he could save Linter from poverty and ignorance, from being trodden and demolished with no chance to manifest God's plan for him! So, he bravely faced the old lady's curse, anger and sarcasm. He determined to make her believe in his sincerity if it would take a hundred visits. He finally won the battle by his persistent patience and kindness. He conquered ignorance with sincerity. The old lady was finally ashamed. She entrusted her grandson to my father's loving care, and she herself eventually became a devout Christian.

Through the inspiration of my father's magnificent love, Linter became a man of great usefulness. During his educational career, he proved to be a man of high caliber and creative mind. Until the influence of my father's unconditional and uncalculated affection and protection, Linter was like a neglected seed thrown in a waterless, barren land; incidentally, he was picked up, transplanted, and watered by a diligent sower. The seed began to bloom into charming flowers. The presence of my father's love in his life was as warm as sunshine. He loved him as dearly as a tender mother would; he educated him strictly, as an authentic father should. Linter was raised in my parents' home and lived with us from the elementary grades till he finished his university education. He became an integral part of our family, acting like an elder brother. We all respected him and called him Tai-kwo-kwo, which means "big brother" in Chinese. My parents tried their best to make him happy and make him forget that he was an orphan. My father's Christian concern had inspired him to live according to God's plan. My father's sacrificial spirit had changed the destiny of Linter from the status of a helpless orphan in a ragged hut to one of the outstanding leaders of the Episcopal Church in China. He received his BA degree from Boone University and his advanced degree in Theology in America and Canada. He became the presiding bishop of Anhui-Kiangsi Diocese and also of Ho-Nai Diocese, up in the north of China. He has been acclaimed as one of the most eminent ministers in China. His linguistic excellence won him overwhelmingly popularity and fame in China, and also while in America and Canada.

My father was particularly proud of Linter and his achievement. He considered Linter as a priceless fruit he had borne during his ministry in Anhui Diocese. Linter's case is often cited as an example to emulate to other children in the family.

YUEH YING'S STORY

Yueh Ying was a charming and lovely girl. When she was eight, her parents were too poor to raise her. They decided to sell her to a nightclub where she would be trained to be a sing-song girl, and eventually become a professional prostitute. This was the only outlet that the parents knew of to solve their heavy financial problem. The incident happened in Kiukiang Kiangsi Province, when my father was planting a church there.

When this was conveyed to my father's ears by one of the church members, his heart was heavily saddened. He felt that he must do something to save this innocent soul. Otherwise, Yueh Ying would certainly fall into the depths of sinful darkness for the rest of her life. The result would be unthinkably tragic. So, my father immediately went with a church member to see Yueh Ying's father. He asked the parent not to sell the little girl.

"Reverend Li, we are desperately poor. We cannot let the child starve to death! What other better way is there to help my child?" Yueh Ying's father sobbed. The mother and Yueh Ying also burst out in convulsive cries, my father told me.

My father looked at this lovely little creature and thought of the cruel poverty that would rob her of parental protection and her right to human dignity and decency. What a pathetic reality! Should he let this problem pass and see the little girl sold in the human market like a piece of commercial goods in the hands of wicked people? My father pondered this gravely, and then resorted to God in solitude and asked for His wisdom and guidance.

God then gave my father the sudden insight and courage to face this case. He returned to Yueh Ying's father. "The first step, Mr. Chu, you must not sell the child to the nightclub because it is a place full of sinful people. I ask you to raise her temporarily. I will advise you what concrete plan we shall arrange to help you."

My father always made big decisions alone with God. He decided that he must help this girl by all means, unhesitatingly. He went to his colleagues and also his best American friend, the Reverend Lund, and told them that if the church could not offer help in this tragic case, he himself would bring Yueh Ying home and raise her as his foster daughter, even though, at that time, my parents already had several children.

The Reverend Lund, a very upright and generous minister in Anhui-Kiangsi Diocese, had participated in many pioneer works with my father. He and my father were very close. He too was deeply impressed and moved by the pitiful case. He responded generously. He said, "I wish I could see this girl." So Yueh Ying was taken to see the Reverend and Mrs. Lund. When they saw her, they loved her at first sight. Yueh Ying's charm and pleasant, smiling face conquered their hearts. Both were eager to have a daughter, for they only had two sons. They anticipated that this new addiction to the family would promote a happier atmosphere, because they were sure that their young sons would enjoy the companionship of a new elder sister.

After a family conference, the Lund family agreed to accept Yueh Ying into their home, and to live as one of the family. Mrs. Lund came to inform my parents of their decision. It was a magnificent decision—to decide to take a poor little girl of another family and of another race into the bosom of their own family! This revealed how God's principle in the Lund family. And it meant transfer into an extremely different world for Yueh Ying.

My father was overcome with grateful joy. He said that he knelt on his knees thanking God in silent prayer. Yueh Ying's parents were inspired by my father's sympathy and by the unrestrained spirit of love that animated the Lunds. The Chu family were all converted and became faithful Christians, because they visualized the grace of God through the shining Christian actions of those two great ministers. "Come thou, ye heavy-laden, I will grant ye peace"; "A heavy and contrite heart, thou shalt not despise": these great promises were kept. How deep was their meaning and how realistic they seemed to Yueh Ying's and her parent's destiny!

At the age of eight, Yueh Ying's life began to move in a wholesome direction. She was officially adopted and named Grace Lund. She was raised in the loving kindness of the Lund family through childhood and adolescence until she became a graceful lady. She had regained the right to live as a decent and dignified human being. I remember when I was small, I was invited to visit the Lunds. The servants called Grace "Tai Shao Chui," which means, "The eldest miss."

She was trained to be a nurse in Wuchang General Hospital (an Episcopal hospital) after finishing high school. There she met my brother David, who was attending Boone University in Wuchang at the time. They fell in love and married—and so finally Yueh Ying also became a member of the Li Family. These two families—Lund and Li—are related in a beautiful yet mysterious way.

WANG DOO-EN'S STORY

Doo-En was a fatherless child from his baby days. His mother was often very sick. She depended on his brother, who was an elementary-school teacher of the church in a rural district of Anhui Province named Fan-chang, when my father was serving there. When Doo-En was ten years old, his mother and brother both died. A year later, his widowed sister-in-law married again, and he was left helpless.

Here was another opportunity for my father to offer help. My parents invited the poor boy to our home and treated him as their own child, notwithstanding the fact that they had two grown sons and three teenage daughters. At that time, I was nine, the youngest of the family, and studying in the same church school as Doo-En. My two elder sisters were studying at a Methodist girls' high school, in Nanking, then capital of China.

This was a hard decision for my father to make. His income was meager, and he had his own children to support, yet mother and he decided to add one more poor child to the family. This involved not only financial responsibility but a long-range educational plan as well. It took a great sacrificial spirit and a generous heart to include the poor and needy one to our family's private life. My father was always willing to help the poverty-stricken and the underprivileged. He and mother had to exercise thrift to raise this child.

My mother usually altered my brothers' and my father's clothing to fit Doo-En. My parents trained us to live understandingly with needy and lonesome people, so that a generous and sacrificial spirit would be unconsciously absorbed by them through realistic contacts. My father's generous love and his endless desire to help others also became deeply rooted in his children's nature.

Doo-En was sent to study at St. James High School, where my eldest brother was the principal. He finished his university education at Boone University. He was very talented in English literature and served as private secretary to the president of the university. He was highly regarded by his professors and the president, and was privileged to study in the United States. Eventually, he was happily married to a schoolmate, Miss Lee, who is a very talented musician.

Doo-En is no longer lonesome and needy. Through my father he was taught Christian vitality and optimism, and to look beyond his childhood miseries.

The aforementioned life stories are only three out of hundreds that were influenced by the affectionate deeds of my father. In everyday life, he sought out and grasped firmly every opportunity to help. He wanted less fortunate people to see God's sunshine and to feel His blessings. Wearing a simple black cotton gown and cotton shoes, he climbed hills and walked over rough roads, with his eyes always searching for lonesome and miserable creatures whom he could help.

He was busy every day of his life. He didn't care much for old-age passions. He prayed to God to teach him how to count his days in this world wisely. He wanted to help others to live; to inspire others to live meaningfully in God's way. This was his highest ideal in life.

It is a very satisfying experience for a person to see what he has sown grow to be a sturdy and well-rooted plant, bearing fruit a hundredfold. The same feeling affected my father he saw the fruitful harvest of his spiritual farming. His dynamic and self-sacrificing way of doing good deeds was really beautiful; his self-effacing way of achieving such good tasks was inspiring as well.

AN UNTIRING
PEDAGOGUE

6

MY FATHER INDUSTRIOUSLY EXPANDED HIS work of spiritual farming. Simultaneously, he worked as a miner, in the sense that he was keenly interested in digging out human treasure. With bountiful enthusiasm and modesty, he was ever eager to educate the younger generation.

In 1899, when he was twenty-eight years of age, he began to open schools for the church. He himself taught Chinese and English, the Bible and arithmetic. Bravely and happily, he shouldered the significant task of educating young minds. Educational work was regarded by the ancient Chinese saints as "a hundred years' responsibility in the cultivating of human trees."

The following passage is translated from a letter from Reverend H. H. Rowe, a student of my father's:

In addition to opening free schools here and there, Reverend Li opened the St. James Academy in Wuhu, Anhui, in 1899, which has been a leading influence in uplifting the cultural and moral standards of Anhui Province. During that pioneer period, there were about a hundred students recruited from different cities and districts, and some even from the most secluded villages of the Province. The turnout at that difficult initial stage was marvelous. It was accredited to the inspiring personality and persistent spirit of the searcher! The parent of the students, although they were conservative, skeptical and most of them illiterate, had confidence in Reverend Li and entrusted their sons' future to the hands of the pioneer educator....

My teacher, Reverend Li, disciplined each of his students like a strict father, and loved each of his students like a merciful mother. Everyone respected him and feared him. Whenever he discovered a worthy talent among the students, he never failed to help him to pursue higher education, and sent him to Boone University in Hupei Province. Those who were financially needy, or with lower scholastic potentiality, were guided to receive technical training in the hospital. He was always alert in discovering, guiding, and following up the individual inclination and needs of each student. Among church members, when he found someone who has really devout and of good moral character, he often assisted him to study in the Theological Seminary of Hankow, or Hankow Normal School, in Hupei Province. After being trained, these members become ministers or teachers for their affiliated church....

His efforts were unsparing to expand the educational work of the church, for he liked to see the barren lands become green pastures, the ignorant become enlightened, empty brains become thinking minds. Wherever his feet trod, there were new schools and new churches, in province, city, district or village. For he held that Christianity enlightens the mind; it is a religion of great wisdom and of positive reasoning. It is not its purpose to indoctrinate people with superstitious beliefs and dogmas. Christianity should help each nation, each state, and each community to train able and righteous members and leaders to bear the abundant fruits of goodness.

My father's method was to stress personal magnetism and moral attraction between teacher and student. He believed discussion essential, and that the relation between student and teacher should be founded on sincerity of heart and friendly benevolence.

Undeniably, throughout his life, he loved his church members, poor or rich, famous or not. He treasured his students. To emphasize this, I will quote another passage from a letter of one of his students:

My teacher, Reverend Li, treated me and each of his students with sincere benevolence. No, not only in words, but by his realistic and sincere actions. The most obvious example was, whenever any one of us would leave Wuhu (Anhui) for Hankow (Hupei) to go to school or returned from school, he would go himself to see him off, or to welcome him back home. During that time, the steamer was usually anchored in the middle of the Yangtze River, not by the river bank. The little *sampan* was the only common means to take the passengers up and down from the bigger steamers. Reverend Li, my dear teacher, worried lest the young people might not be careful enough, and might slip off their feet and thus endanger their lives, so he made sure to be with them going to and from the steamer. The steamer sailed downward from Hupei to Wuhu, usually arriving around daybreak. Summer or winter, hot or cold, fair or stormy weather, he waited at the pier at the river for his beloved students! From this touching example, one can realize how sincerely he was concerned with his students, just as dearly as with his own sons. His immeasurable affection and graciousness were engraved deeply and unforgettably in the grateful hearts of all his students!

His enthusiasm for teaching the rising generation won him respect and admiration as the outstanding educator of his time. In 1907 my father was elected as a delegate of all churches to the World Educational Conference, held in Japan and sponsored by the world YMCA.

Throughout his whole lifetime, he was profoundly absorbed in educating young people to be useful Christian leaders. Also, he himself constantly enriched his own knowledge by studying prodigiously. He advised us: "To pursue knowledge is like rowing a boat upstream; if you don't push forward hard, your scholarship will automatically go backward. It can never stand still." During my earliest childhood, I began to respect my father as an assiduous learner.

Wherever he went, he was surrounded by a group of learners. He taught them not only worldly knowledge, not only how to grow intellectually, but, above all, to build up a wholesome outlook on life, and to seek freedom through the truth of God for the service of mankind.

His students often called him "our mother," because he loved and cared for each one much like a mother. I remember that during summer vacations or Chinese New Year my home was full of visiting students of my father. They loved to spend their vacations with my parents. All of them were treated like family folks. All of the male student were my big brothers, and the female students were my big sisters.

When I was a tiny girl, I was impressed by the fact that not only were my parents busy with their own routine work, but also entertained and looked after their students. They loved all of them and the students' children too. My mother told me that during the Ching Dynasty, before the establishment of the Nationalist Government, men wore queues. Every morning, she had to arrange the braids of my two big brothers, and Brother Linter Tseng, Brother Tai, and Brother Rowe, my father's students living in our home.

Watching over the coming and goings of the lively young people were a great delight in the life of my parents. They were never too tired to join in the activities of the students living with them. Their lives were deeply involved in the lives of the younger generation whom they treasured so dearly. Confucius says: "Guide the disciples untiringly and incessantly." And this applies to my father's guidance methods. He lived with each student and watched him grow toward a wholesome direction in life.

Even during his old age, he did not become absorbed in himself. He kept alive his love and interest in others, who tied him to life. Like Paul, he was always looking forward; he knew that a useful and abundant life meant a life in which there is always much to be accomplished in the future.

Li Yuanmo and his wife (date of photo unknown).

Li Zhaowen and his wife (date of photo unknown). Li Zhaowen is the eldest son of Li Yuanmo, the big brother of Ellen Li Juan.

St. Jacob's Church in Wuhu, Anhui Province, China, first built in 1883, renovated in 2005 by local government (date of photo unknown).

Ellen Li Juan (date of photo unknown).

THE CHILDREN'S RECORD OF LOVE

7

MY FATHER IMPLANTED LOVE AND GRACE IN HIS children. His tender affection was as eternal as the sun and the moon, as far-reaching and as deeply penetrating as the sky and the sea! Every word he spoke, every little deed he did had an invisible but vital and directing force upon his children and served to renew strength and vitality in their lives.

Father was born in 1871, in an old-fashioned Chinese agricultural community. People were mostly, if not all, conservative and aristocratic-minded, especially in their attitude toward women, which was characterized by the traditional convention that men are superior and women inferiors. The greatest virtue a woman could possess was submissiveness—submission to her father when she was a girl, to her husband during her married life, and to her son when she was old. But my father was a fair and democratic-minded person. His thinking and his spirit were as modern as today's youth. Toward my mother, toward each of his children, he appeared as a man with a beautiful nature. In the daily contacts of our family life, we children could sense that my father was a wonderful husband to my mother.

My mother told me that my father was a most a most considerate lifetime companion, and a very faithful husband. My mother had been parentless since she was nine years of age, and besides taking care of herself, she brought up her younger brother. She was born and grew up in the same village as my father. Recommended by a mediator, she was engaged to my father at the age of ten.

In the old days, especially in Chinese rural communities, girls were matched when very young to boys of corresponding social background by the consent and agreement of parents or guardians. There was also a custom in China that when a girl became engaged, she went to live in her fiancé's family as a "waiting bride" or "waiting daughter-in-law." My mother came to live with my grandfather's family when she was twelve, and was wed to my father when she was nineteen. It was a tremendously complicated adjustment for a young child to make. She was wise and industrious, and dutiful to my grandfather. My mother said that she was devoted to my grandfather, and was regarded by him as the most virtuous and lovable daughter-in-law among his three sons' wives.

During my mother's girlhood, Chinese girls were not allowed to enter school; they had no chance at all for formal education. After she was married, mother said that my father taught her to read the Bible and the prayer book. My father's love and compassion had compensated and substituted for the parental affection she had never had because of the early loss of her parents. For instance, father had two important duties to perform upon awakening each morning: one was to pray alone in his study at daybreak; the other was to make a pot of delicious green tea for my mother. He insisted on making the tea himself, not allowing the servant to do it. He did this unfailingly until a few days before he departed this world. It is a touchingly loving memory that never dies in the hearts of his loved ones.

Although he was busy the year round with church and school activities, he was always considerate to my mother in every way. Gentle and sincerely modest were my father's manners toward my mother. Every evening, at family prayer my father never failed to pray for my mother. In his devout prayer, he said: "May the dear Lord bless the children's mother always and keep her in good health and happiness," is and ever shall be remembered in each of his children's heart. His inspiring praying voice was unchangeable over several decades toward my mother and is still affectionately recalled by his children!

It is a common everyday experience to encounter in human society aggressive and selfish persons. It also happens within families, where disputes, disagreements, and disillusionments among husbands and wives are often due to lack of affectionate mutual appreciation and respect. Mistreatment, mistrust, or angry words over financial and other material matters have often led to the disintegration of a happy family life. And dysfunctional and unhealthy family relationships have consequently blocked social progress.

My father loved my mother with an affectionate concern and respect, a manner the very opposite to that of the self-centered husband who abuses and dominates his wife. My father gave my mother credit and appreciation for whatever she did for the children and for him. He sympathized with my mother, who was so virtuous, thrifty, industrious, and devotion toward the family. Throughout her life, she realized that her responsibility was to help her husband and to educate her children. I am very thankful to God for giving me wonderful parents who built up their relationship on mutual respect and consideration, and that I was brought up in a harmonious atmosphere. For example, my father always handed over his monthly income to my mother to be spent at her discretion on the family. He was not a bit selfish or dominating in financial matters. Although I was very young, I still remember my father giving my mother the salary remittance on the first day of each month, usually in silver coins. "Your father is a wonderful man," my mother often said to us. His action shows that my father had complete confidence and high regard for my mother's authority in the family, unlike many husbands of today and yesterday who act like dictators, especially where the family finances are concerned, with angry quarrels and resentful wives the inevitable result. The fact is—and was—very true in any conservative society, particularly in nineteenth-century China.

My father was not only concerned with my mother's physical welfare; he also cared for her soul and her spiritual health. During our daily family prayers, every member of the family as well as the servants were required to attend. We took turns reading Bible verses. My mother was often invited to read and to answer questions. Even when I was very young, I realized that my mother was a highly intelligent woman. With no education at all, yet she read well and expressed her thoughts clearly. My father constantly instilled in her God's wisdom. He was a good companion in her daily life, a nurse during her sickness, a comforter in her distress. His warmth and kindness made her forget her solitary destiny. Thus my mother lived happily and courageously because of my father's devotion.

To the children, my father was tender, kind, and gracious. Down the long range of my memories, I always see him with an inspiring smile, and I always hear his tenderly persuasive voice in my inner life.

My parents begot ten children, six daughters and four sons. I was the tenth child, the youngest in the family. Five of my brothers and sisters died when they were very young, from one cause or another.

My father tried his very best to give every possible advantage to his children and to develop in each the natural gifts that God had bestowed. Although he was very busy, yet he never for a moment forgot his children. He was enthusiastically concerned with the moral, intellectual, physical, and social development of all of them. During the daily family worship periods he taught us to grasp the priceless biblical precepts and the wisdom of God. This exerted a far-reaching influence upon our moral growth. Father believed that we should not rely solely upon the material facts of knowledge and science we learned in school for our guidance, that we must let the great supreme power of God guide us from within.

Throughout his entire life, he was exceedingly absorbed in developing in us the virtue of benevolence, and he held it to be the motivating force that promotes true happiness in human relationships, the yeast that unites the whole world in lasting peace. To exist selfishly, without benevolent regard for others, is to lead an aimless life. My father also taught us that, to exist in this world, the enrichment of knowledge is important, but that more important than the mere accumulation of knowledge is to know the ultimate aim of the acquisition of knowledge, that is, to be wholesome and useful member of society, ever ready to contribute to the common good of mankind. To a person with a lot of knowledge but lacking sturdy will power, the acquired knowledge is useless and dead. A brave person of ardent spirit who nevertheless possesses an empty mind will find no way to manifest his desire for benevolent actions. So, my father's philosophy of education stressed the blending of materialistic scientific knowledge with the Christian spirit. He endeavored to train us to be persons with well-informed minds, the power of self-discipline and moral control, persistent and sturdy willpower, sincere and honest character, and a personality that exemplified a harmonious integration of Christian virtues with the great ethical ideals of the Chinese cultural heritage. He encouraged us to learn to be persons possessing lofty ideals, irresistible, unconquerable, and magnificent in our moral strength, and sublime in our wisdom.

He was the one who taught me to think, to speak, to read, and to act intelligently from the time I was tiny. When I was very small, my father always found time to teach me to read useful books, the Chinese classics, and newspaper editorials. He taught me how to use a brush to write the Chinese characters when I was seven. He also taught me how to compose and organize ideas, and to speak in public. His inspirational guidance aroused in me a profound interest in searching for knowledge and helped to build a solid foundation for my academic education in later years. He helped each one of us to develop self-confidence and self-reliance by positive encouragement; he never let us be discouraged or develop conditions of failure. Ever since my childhood, I have been thankful that I often won first place in my class. I received my elementary school education in St. Lioba's Convent of the Episcopal Church, and my secondary education at Hwei Wen Methodists Girls' School, in Nanking. I received prizes, awards, and a scholarship grant every year. My father and mother were very happy and proud of my achievements. During my senior year in high school, I won the honor award for outstanding scholastic achievements. The award was a scholarship of seventeen silver dollars. My parents were so thrilled that tears of joy came to their eyes when I handed my mother the award money. During my college years in Yenching University, I studied hard, with ardent spirit. I ranked as one of the top students, and was graduated with the honor of the Golden Key. For all these successes, I must acknowledge my deepest indebtedness to my father's constant interest and inspirational guidance.

To each of his children, he was as tender and as affectionate as my mother. When I was a tiny child, he came to my bedside every evening and taught me to pray. "Have you prayed?" was often his question. The short little prayer, "I shall have a peaceful sleep for the dear Lord abides with me," was the first prayer my father taught me. It is remembered forever with deep affection and sweet thoughts. Even now, no matter where I am, I close my eyes at bedtime and the little soothing prayer flows from my heart like a murmuring voice, spontaneously. After I finish praying, all worldly cares and burdens are lessened, or slide off into nothingness.

During the night, my father would get up to make sure we were warmly covered by our blankets, so that we would not catch a cold. When we were sick, he waited on us and comforted us as mother did. His kind hands would touch the burning head of his sick child, or he would give us medicine or take our temperature. He loved each of us dearly and abundantly. He fostered our physical and spiritual development, day by day.

While I was studying in the boarding school in Nanking, and later, while at Yenching University, in Peiping, my father, in each of his letters, stressed that I must take good care of myself physically, and above all, read the Bible daily to learn to be a devout Christian, and a shining Christian example to my fellow schoolmates.

He was a great father. He stood side by side with my mother, and the two of them guided each of their children. Whenever we had personal difficulties, whether big or small, serious or not, he always would pat us on the shoulder and say in a soothing, calm voice: "My child, don't worry. Pray to out dear Lord. He will help you to do your best and renew your strength." My father taught us to meet hard problems calmly, and we could then achieve success through the wisdom and courage from God without unnecessary nerve strain. He always urged us to mold our lives into a beautiful and triumphant pattern. His everlasting love has left imperishable and charming traces in our hearts.

His method of educating his children was practical. He taught us to love and sympathize with the poor and needy by having us actually live with them—by housing underprivileged and lonesome children in our own home. My father loved us but he never indulged us. He was strict but he was not unreasonably compelling. He was tolerant but he never spoiled us. His teaching was so inspirational that it had a penetrating and direct effect on a child's reasoning power, and led to self-discipline. He was always stressed the goal of self-betterment.

The following instance illustrates my father's educational methods. During the period of 1915–1921, he was working in Kiangsi Province, organizing churches and opening schools. In 1922 he was appointed by Bishop Hungtington to lead the Chinese Christian movement in Anhui-Kiangsi Diocese, carrying the evangelistic campaign into every rural district of these two provinces in central China. He traveled over the entire diocese. His work involved much moving about from one place to another, so our family had to move from Kiangsi Province to Wuhu, in Anhui Province.

Two months before the big move, Mr. Wang, a member of the Kiukiang Episcopal Church who respected my father highly, entrusted his only son, Wang Tao, with my parents for study at St. James High School, which had been founded by my father. One summer evening, during suppertime, my second sister, then ten years old, said innocently to Wang Tao, who was about my sister's age, "Are you going with us to Wuhu?" Wang said yes. "Your luggage and bedding are heavy. They will take up a lot of room on the steamer, and it will cost a lot of money to take you to Wuhu," said my sister.

My father heard this childish chat and it provoked a stern reaction. He was annoyed by my sister's careless but innocent comments. He spanked her severely.

My sister, punished in the severest manner she had ever experienced, burst into tears. Deeply sympathizing with my dear sister, who was my closest companion, I cried too. My mother's tender heart was also hurt; she cried likewise. The whole family was in agony of tears, fear, and silent sympathy. We all, including Wang Tao and the maidservant, thought that my father had been too severe with my dear sister.

My father emphasized the qualities of moral goodness and benevolent affection more than anything else. He had punished my sister because she had spoken unkind, unfriendly, and hurtful words, lacking in the proper benevolent and cooperative spirit, to a friend in her home. He said: "When a friend or a relative is living with us, we must treat him with sincere hospitality and friendly love. We should not use hurtful or stinging words, or show a hypocritical heart, to a friend and hurt his feeling. We must make others feel at home and share every happy moment with them. You are young, but if you are selfish, and unfeeling to a friend now, when you grow up, what use will you be to others? Would you like others to treat you the same way you treat them?" After saying this, my father went indignantly to his study room and shut the door. All of us went to bed with heavy hearts that night. The whole family was deeply impressed by my father's anger and his exhortation.

But when my sister and I broke his precious thirty-year collection of antique Chinese porcelain vases, he demonstrated his kindness and tolerance! I was only six, and I remember that my sister and I were so frightened and anticipated severe punishment for our careless behavior. We wandered around the church grounds the whole day, not daring to face our parents. My mother worried about where we might be and searched for us with the maid, until we were found under a pine tree on the hill opposite the church grounds. We two sinful little creatures went back with my mother, with restless and fear-stricken consciences. We confessed our bad behavior in front of our father. He was not angry at all, but he said: "I forgive you this time. But you little children must not forget this serious lesson—from now on you must be very careful in handling things entrusted to you by others."

His precepts and lessons were deeply engraved on our hearts. They still exert an invisible influence.

Now, as I tread along on life's journey, I hate cruelty, hypocrisy, selfish, and spiritual mistreatment. I love righteousness, generosity, and consideration for others. These were rooted in me by my father's inspirational guidance when I was young.

He constantly sought to inculcate in us the moral strength to repel the evil forces of this materialistic age. He trained us to be kind and sympathetic toward the heart-stricken and the miserable, and and taught us that our heart should contact and treat someone else's heart with loving consideration and appreciation. He helped us to build up an inner understanding and concern for others, and for any worthwhile human cause. He taught us good taste and a love of simplicity, and he gave me a well-directed ambition which forever supplies valuable incentives for true and decent living. All these priceless virtues and spiritual possessions came to me intuitively from my father, little by little, in the course of our daily life.

Throughout his whole life, he guided his children and his children's children firmly and lovingly along pathways that led to a meaningful and beautiful pattern of life. He taught us to find the source of real beauty, goodness and justice, which is God himself. He used great thoughts, precepts, and deeds to strengthen the delicate young minds and souls of his loved ones.

INCESSANT BATTLES

8

MY FATHER'S NOBLE CHARACTER AND KIND HEART impressed others in much the same way that one is gladdened by breathing the fragrance of a white rose. It gives a sensation of calm and sublime beauty. Or, as when one is in the presence of a lamb, one is bound to forget the cruelty in the world.

He was not an artist, yet he was not satisfied with the material realities. He was concerned with the cultivation of his conception of man's place in the world. Like great musicians and writers, he was forever joyful and thankful to God for giving him the power to create, to work toward perfect goodness and purity. He observed things analytically, with an artist's eye, when he considered human activities and affairs. He was ever positive and vital in seeking the goodness and beauty of life. He proclaimed that genuine and absolute goodness and beauty originated only from God the Creator.

In the course of seeking righteousness, he was firm and daring. As in boyhood, he consistently refused to accept contemporary superstitious beliefs. He would not kneel before a clay Buddha. He often chose the narrow way, the bitter way, to seek the sublime ideal of life. He ventured to fight against all sorts of environmental handicaps; he was not disheartened by failure or by the disdain of others. He conquered every difficulty with his unshakable faith and Christian optimisim. He won his first evangelical battle with his beloved father. He converted his father to Christianity, and the elder man experienced "rebirth" to a glorious new life. He has erected a milestone in the history of religious faith in his father's family. And he achieved this not by force or words but by action—the great virtue of filial obedience and immense love!

My grandfather—a very conservative old man—had been a Buddhist throughout his lifetime. Later, after he became a Christian, he was with my father for most of the rest of his life, until he left this world. He considered his life blissful and felicitous, for he had enjoyed the fullest filial respect and obedience from both my parents, who kept his heart forever young and joyful during his declining years. He forgot the laborious and strenuous life of his past. The love in the Chinese family between son and father, children and parents, is one of the firmest and least disputed of Chinese traditions. Chinese children are dutybound to support their parents. Chinese parents, when old, particularly if widowed, always live with their sons and daughters, married or not. In China, aged parents do not have to worry about living alone in hotels, apartments, or sitting alone on park benches, as I have seen them in Boston and New York, or to spend their declining years in an old people's home. Their sons and daughters, their grandchildren, and even relatives are willing to offer them affectionate care. Being a daughter-in-law, my mother was also deeply imbued with China's family-love caring tradition and held her aged father-in-law in high respect. She was very proud of having a loving father-in-law who rocked the crib for his grandchildren with the same loving kindness that he had given to his own sons. My mother also told me that my grandfather had baby-sat for his grandchildren. Five days before he left this world, he rocked his second grandson.

The Chinese respect for the aged is a tribute to their wisdom and experience, which they hand down to the younger generation. Custom and filial obedience are two major moral factors that link the Chinese younger generation happily together with the aged parents living under the same roof with them. Through four thousands of years of Chinese history, we have recognized the importance of truth and unselfishness in the whole wide field of human relations as they are connected with the great virtue of filial piety.

Christianity is complementary to this great virtue as set forth in one of the Ten commandments: "Honor thy father and thy mother, that your days may be long." This was proved to be true by my grandfather, because his son and daughter-in-law held filial obedience to be so important in their way of living with the widower father. My father often reflected on what his father once said: "My son is a teacher, a minister; he is not a rich man. But I have enjoyed the greatest possible comfort and bliss given by him and his wife. They have paid greater filial obedience to me than have selfish rich people who show so little spiritual gratitude to their parents."

Affectionate love and filial piety were constantly present in the life of my grandfather. During his declining years, his faith in Buddhism weakened and he was inspired by Christianity.

In 1900 the Boxer Rebellion dealt a serious blow to religious work in China. It was an anti-foreigner's revolt, and blocked the expansion of Christian evangelism activities. All missionaries and their families were evacuated and took refuge in the foreign concession in Shanghai. My father brought the whole family to Shanghai. My grandfather was very sick at this time. My parents were completely devoted to the aged man. My mother said that during the critical days he could not even get up to go to the toilet and frequently soiled the bedding. My father thought it would be too inconvenient for my mother to nurse him, since she had several young children to take care of, for my eldest brother and second brother were very small at that time. Linter Tseng was also with our family. My father changed and bathed and nursed his father, day and night. At the critical moment of his life, his tears of pride and love flowed freely. He was content at heart, because he was deeply impressed by his son and his daughter-in-law's sincere love and respect. At the last, he requested my father to christen him with holy water, as he wanted to receive salvation for his soul before returning to his heavenly home. He was happy, relaxed, and triumphant.

The battle against superstitious belief was regarded by my father as the most significant and glorious page in the record of his fight for Truth and Righteousness. He held that, to be a Christian soldier, one must first educate oneself; second, one must regulate his family; and then he can spread the battle to society, the nation, and the whole world.

Undeniably, he was alert, firm, and brave in standing on the path of Righteousness and everlasting Truth of God. My father realized that because a person stands firmly for righteousness it does not necessarily imply that he should adopt passivism and pessimism, as Buddhism holds, to escape worldly pursuits. Christianity is a religion of positive actions, of constant battle against the evils and the selfish desires of humanity. A Christian must struggle through darkness in order to reach light. Godly people should not fearfully surrender to the crowd of wicked people around them, or be tricked by them, thus cutting the thread that links good to good and results in shutting up the good people in a blind alley. No longer able to march forward toward freedom and truth, their plight could endanger all society, and the whole world could sink into darkness.

So, my father realized that when we are living in a time of twisted truths, we cannot rely on someone's limited wisdom for peace and happiness. We must modestly and persistently seek wisdom and righteousness from the inner power and heroism of great men, and endeavor to build self-discipline, and acknowledge the judgment of God. Throughout his whole life, when my father dealt with people and their problems, he faced them bravely and heroically. A Chinese proverb says: "Be brave to do good deeds." Whenever my father saw that the thing to do was a righteous thing, he did it fearlessly.

His firm and upright individuality was matched by his modest, sincere character, his love for truth, and his hatred of cupidity. He was always ready to fight for a lofty ideal of life. Floating no matter where he might be found, working for what he believed in, he encountered many bitter experiences. But he loved God's righteousness, he was quite satisfied with his limited material possessions. He never complained over setbacks. He was neither proud of any success he achieved nor discouraged by failure. He did not care for worldly pleasures and modern extravagances. All he wanted was spiritual achievement. Because he was self-sufficient with his limited material possessions, he actualized the virtue of thrift. He learned self-control by living simply, resisting every temptation to accumulate wealth and fame. He focused his entire energy and God's power within him on worthy causes. His inner peace and security came from God, the Almighty Father. Thus his spiritual reward was a thousand fold richer, and his wisdom more abundant than any millionaires.

He was strong-willed in regard to what he believed. He realized that to mold the human heart, to cultivate a beautiful soul, and to help others to live abundantly were works of ever-lasting value, works to which it was worthwhile to dedicate his entire resourcefulness, therefore turned down many prominent positions that would have him a higher income than did a minister's job. My father was widely recognized as a man of superior intelligence, a highly and capable leader. He was offered many such attractive opportunities. He told me that he had been offered the office of postmaster in the Hupei Provincial Government, but he was not interested, and flatly declined the offer. He believed what the Bible says: "Seek ye first the kingdom of God and his righteousness, all the rest will be added unto you."

With a choice of many more lucrative occupations, he chose to be a spiritual farmer, sowing the seeds of God's truth and righteousness among men. He turned his back on many opportunities that would have brought him material prosperity and fame, preferring to devote himself to God's righteousness and help men and women realize the ideal of human brotherhood. His ideals were often ridiculed by selfish and arrogant people as being as vague and unrealistic as moonlight on the water, or as unrealizable as castles in the air. Some laughed at his ideals and called them empty bubbles. In this apathetic age, it would be difficult to find another hero who had such ambitious ideals to fight for! In this bewildering and chaotic world of ugly intrigue, nation vies with nation, individual struggles with individual and every country in the world is filled with terror and deadly gloom. These conditions are created by human selfishness, the ambition of some greedy men to advance themselves at the expense of their brethren. Contemplating this age of moral dependence, I ponder whether we do need a mass production of such heroic and fearless fighter and Christian as my humble father. He tried to start a moral awakening and spiritual reformation for generating mankind.

He always insisted on faith. He firmly held that to rely on God's wisdom in life is far more priceless the precious gems of this world. Only God knows the path of righteousness, and He alone is the source of pure wisdom. Seeking this source of Godly wisdom in order to pursue a beautiful and true life, my father was always alert to maintain his firm stand on righteousness. He learned from God's precepts to be a great man.

UNCOMPLAINING HEROISM

9

MY FATHER TRAVELED LIFE'S VOYAGE FOR EIGHTY-ONE years. He passed through innumerable vicissitudes, analogous to the fluctuations of the deep sea. He tasted to the full both the sweet and the acrid experiences of human living. His life was enriched by his wide contacts and constant struggles during his active years. Mostly, life's pathway, for him, was narrow and steep.

The richest life is often one that is tinged with bitter experiences. The beauty of a really rich life is sometimes crystallized by the heat of harsh encounters. Beethoven proclaimed a great truth to those who have ears to hear. In his *Pastoral Symphony*, he began to write about the shepherd's happiness that a storm is over. But the Supreme Creator of all inspiration took over the composer's pen. That simple shepherd's melody became a mighty paean of joy, echoing from crag to crag, swelling from mountain to mountain top, with all the creatures of earth swinging into a dance of rapture, and the stars of heavens bursting forth in song. An overwhelming tide of thankfulness sweeps over the great man as he realized that God is good, the world is beautiful, and men divine despite the bitter storm of life. The same kind of immensity of spiritual power was within my father's soul!

Thumbing over the pages of my father's diary, I found many things to admire in that heroic man. He viewed bad and good luck as if they were the right and the left hand of his body; and he made good use of both. At the age of five, he lost his mother. He was therefore denied to know the love of a kind mother as nearly every child does. The loss of a mother's divine love is a blow to a child's delicate soul, no matter how unconsciously it may be felt. There is an undeniable spiritual hollowness in the heart that no substitute can fill. In my father's case, this was the first storm in his life.

Marching like a Christian crusader through the wilderness of a world full of chaos, he sought God's righteousness, fighting for truth and justice. He was frequently attacked by selfish and arrogant hypocrites and subjected to insult, sarcasm, and disdain. The more obstacles he was confronted with, the more intensively he carried on his battle against evil. He tried to realize God's will here on earth. He had been tremendously afflicted. He often said: "Only God knows how heavy my heart is!" He knew that a person with a loving heart is usually aware of the problems and insatiable needs of others, and feels more pain than a selfish person can understand.

But he also recognized that an afflicted heart does not have the courage to steer toward a sweeter, brighter objective in life. He compared a heavy heart to morning dew, which touches every thirsty flower and beautifies it. Likewise genuine tears can cleanse impurities from the human heart, and give it a richer function. Bitter setbacks and afflictions can encourage a person to be more creative, forward-striving. And my father believed God's great promise: "A heavy and contrite heart, thou shalt not despise."

He was a brave man, facing all kinds of personal problems and upheavals heroically. He stood uncomplainingly during the crucial moments of his trials. When his family met with misfortune, he did not tremble. His physical frailty did not discourage him or make him feel pessimistic toward life. He was never strong, not even in full manhood, and constantly suffered from an intestinal disorder. This painful ailment made deep inroads in his physical health. He told me that when he was thirty-six, he was elected delegate by the churches to attend the World Conference on Youth Education, in Japan, sponsored by the YMCA. On his way back, while on shipboard, he was stricken with typhoid and had to be sent to the General Hospital, in Shanghai, when the ship docked. He suffered from the disease for seventy-two days, and before it was over, a rigid diet had reduced him to skin and bones. During the very critical moments, his fever was so high that he was delirious and often lost consciousness. His illness was so severe the doctors held little hope for his recovery. During one of his spells of delirium, he got out of bed and attempted to leap from the window of his hospital room, on the fifth floor. Fortunately, he was caught and saved by the nurse, who came in just in time. At that time, there were only my three older brothers and my oldest sister in the family. Death seemed to be approaching for my father. My mother took the children and went to visit my father in the Shanghai hospital. The American missionary, Reverend Lund, kindly accompanied my mother and the children from Wuhu to Shanghai. My mother was deeply worried and grieved.

A Chinese proverb says: "A human being cannot calculate happenings as adequately as Heaven does." The Bible says (Psalm 118, verses 16–19): *The right hand of the Lord is exalted: the right hand of the Lord doeth valiantly. I shall not die, but live, and declare the works of the Lord. The Lord hath chastened me sore: but he hath not given me over unto death.* "God was good to my father and saved him while he hovered between life and death. This really meant resurrection to my father and his family.

His experience on the bridge between life and death gave my father deeper insights and a new awareness of God's purpose for him. It must have been that God needed him to awaken the nonbelievers from their slumbers. After this serious trial, he more intelligently reckoned his newly added days and months. His strength came back, his fighting enthusiasm intensified, and his faith deepened, for he realized that God must have a plan for him since He saved him from the edge of death. It meant that his work for God was not yet finished, and that he must undertake a prodigious job of expanding Christian works for mankind. So he became busier on God's side than he had ever been before!

My parents had ten children; five of them died either before I was born or when I was too tiny to remember them. My third older brother, my parents said, died of typhoid fever. He was a brilliant and good-natured boy, and my parents loved him dearly. He died one week before he was ten years old. In China, parents usually gave a big birthday party for a child on his tenth, twentieth, thirtieth birthdays. My brother's party had been planned too. My mother had made a beautiful Chinese quilted satin gown for my brother, but it was all in vain! The gown was used as part of the apparel the dead boy wore to God's paradise. How tragic! He died at the moment my father was officiating at the wedding ceremony of his beloved student, C. K. Tai, who became a medical doctor later. My father was not able to see his son during his last moments, when he was leaving forever his loving parents. What a contrast in the two events! In God's house, a happy wedding was held with a happy congregation full of hopeful wishes, and laughter, for the future of the newly wedded couple, while in the house of my parents, a loving child's of war ended his young, green life! His sudden departure saddened my parents' hearts and their tears poured out as if from a fountain. It was unbearable for my mother. Whenever she recalled it, she cried. My father covered up his feelings, and tried to make his student happy while conducting the wedding ceremony. He learned to share two contradictory emotions at the same time: to laugh with the happy couple and the congregation; and concealed his tears as he thought of his lifeless son!

There have been many civil wars in China's history, and several were experienced by my parents. I have already alluded to the Boxer Rebellion, in 1900. The Sino-Japanese War of 1937–1945 was never forgotten by the Chinese people. It was caused by the inhuman aggression, brutality, and selfishness of the Japanese military dictators. The heavy, steady bombardment, the hunger, and robbery, burning, killing, and raping on all sides. These horrors were imposed upon the peace-loving Chinese victims! Many homeless people carried small bundles containing all their possessions, as they sneaked from place to place, as if playing hide-and-seek with the enemy. People from all walks of life, all classes of the social system, and all age groups suffered from this devilish war of aggression. They climbed steep mountains, waded rivers, disregarding whatever horrible weather conditions prevailed. The helpless babies were carried on the backs of parents or grandparents as they walked to freedom! No Chinese wanted to see a Japanese soldier, no one desired to live in shallow peace under a despotic rule. The ruthlessness and savage behavior of the enemy led to hatred deep down in the Chinese people's blood. They wanted freedom at any expense, and no matter what material loss they might suffer. They walked and walked and sought refuge deep in the interior of China, places where only the prints of tigers' paws had been before. Yet they chose to hide there for the sake of peace and personal freedom. Any place to escape from the tyrannical faces of Japanese soldiers. It was a vivid yet unforgettably sad picture in every Chinese mind!

During the World War II, my parents were in their declining years. They were too old either to walk or to endure the anxieties due to the chaotic conditions of evacuation. But they had to leave the occupied areas owing to the heavy bombardment and the lack of food in the Japanese-occupied zones. They left with my second brother Philip and his wife, my second sister, and my brother's five little children. They walked and waded along the Yangtze River from Hupei down to the interior of Kiangsi Province, crossing the mountain of Lu, the former renowned resort for foreign missionaries, and to the interior of Anhui Province, namely, the Mou-Lin district. They encountered a shortage of both food and money. My mother was so weak that she could barely walk. She was carried by my brother over the mountain of Lu. The hardships of this bitter experience left their mark on my aged parents.

But my father endured all this misery calmly and heroically, as another hardship on the voyage of life. During the war, I was suffering in another part of China. I wrote to my parents about the unbearable life of wartime. My father, forgetting his own difficulties, wrote me a letter of consolation that offered me great encouragement, strengthened my courage to strive forward, and calm my nervousness. Part of the letter (translated) is as follows:

...St. Paul could become the greatest disciple of his time, because he had suffered more than his contemporaries. Our great saint, Confucius, rode in a cart drawn by two horses to get around to the different nations of his time. He was arrested by Chan-Tsoi, insulted by Yang-Hu, and satirized by Chee. Although he died with a name of eternal glory, yet he didn't enjoy a moment of happiness in his life.

In the manufacture of tin plate, raw iron must be first subjected to a chemical process, before it becomes polished, rust-proof tinplate. A similar process is true in human experience: God gives us many bitter trials—deaths, disappointments, failures, calamities, wars—to try our patience. As raw iron is transformed by its polished covering when it becomes tinplate, our characters change by suffering, until we can visualize God's rich blessings. We must be trained through hard and bitter lessons of life, so that we may learn to live more usefully and creatively.

Dear child, when we face difficulties and disappointments, pray to God for wisdom. In the present bitter trial we must go through the process of acid action, and finally we will learn that hard lessons are useful for spiritual growth and aggrandizement.

Hebrews 12:5–8 says: "My son, despise not thou the chastening of the Lord, nor faint when thou are rebuked of him: For whom the Lord loveth he chasteneth, and scrougeth every son whom he receiveth. If ye endure chastening, God dealeth with you as with sons; for what son is he whom the father chasteneth not?"

James 1:2–4 says: "Count it all joy when ye fall into divers temptations; Knowing this, that the trying of your faith worketh patience. But let patience have her perfect work, that ye may be perfect and entire, wanting nothing."

We were born in sorrow: this is a universal truth. Mencius said: *"We were born in calamity,"* which means the same as what Job says in Job 14:1.

From all these things we can realize that calamities are inevitable in human life, especially when our country is invaded by enemies, bringing great unrest and misfortune to every citizen of the nation. I hope you, dear child, will face these things patiently and calmly, as we all must now, and share with the whole nation, and her people these tremendously troubled times.

In time of affliction, get closer to God, pray sincerely to God...

When my father was seventy-three and my mother was seventy-one, a succession of tragic events saddened their hearts, one after another. My second brother, Philip Li, who graduated from St. John's University (Episcopal) in Shanghai and had received his ministerial training at the School of Theology there, died. Four months later, my eldest sister, Mildred Li Yang, wife of Reverend Yang, of Hupei Diocese, also died.

My beloved brother died an untimely death. He was just approaching middle age, and his great usefulness was tremendously needed by the church, the school, and his family. He had five dependent children and his wife, the adopted daughter Elizabeth Barber, of Richmond, Virginia, USA, who had been a missionary worker in Anking, Anhui Diocese, for many years. It was a most tragic and heart-rending loss. The night before he died, he sobbed broken-heartedly to his best friend: "The ones I hate to leave in this world are my respectable and aged parents, whose graciousness and love I have no time to repay! Yet, my God wants to take me away first. My children and my wife, though I hold them dearly in my affection, are young and healthy. I trust that God and my relatives will look after them. They will follow the line of their own destiny. Oh, my dear friend, please take good care of my loving and aged parents, and look after them and comfort them for my sake, your poor friend who has no time for love!"

My brother Philip had had a bountiful supply of affection for his older brother and his younger sisters. He was a man of big heart and generous favors. His virtuous character and his touching affection will long be cherished and greatly missed by his folks, his friends, his students, and by his church members.

On the very day of my brother's funeral, my father slipped and fell down. It seems incredible, but God caused his foot to become permanently paralyzed right from that sad day! This misfortune seemed to indicate that God knew how his heart ached as he faced his son's death in his old age. This fall prevented him from even more sadness at seeing the coffin with his beloved grown son within it, and the son's wife and innocent children mourning. How could my tender-hearted, aged parents withstand such a painfully gloomy scene again! God stopped him from going to his son's funeral, but my mother attended and fainted during the service, when the coffin was opened to give her a last farewell glance at her son! It was a calamity that troubled my parents' hearts until they left this world.

Mildred's death, four months later, was another terrifying ordeal. The message from my brother-in-law told us that my sister died of typhoid fever. The day before she died, her fever rose rapidly, and she became delirious. She became difficult to control and movements brought on intestinal bleeding. Her husband and her two-year-old daughter were at her bedside. Her husband, three young sons, and a daughter, survived her.

One after another! My eldest brother, David, had received this news first. It was decided that the news should be kept from my father, and it was a year before it was disclosed to him. My father calmly bowed to God's plan. He prayed and kept the sad news in his heart for another year. Then my mother was informed of it. She shed bitter tears of love. These tragic shocks drove her to a pessimistic melancholia during her declining years, even though the other children tried their very best to fill her heart with devotion and love.

After the death of my second brother, my father's foot became so weak, that he had to walk with the help of a crutch. It was God's plan to weaken his tired feet, which he has used to carry him so many thousand miles in his seventy years of spreading God's message. He was so faithful in seeking God's lost souls for the church that now his tired feet needed a restful change. My father did not doubt God's trials of him; his faith was not shaken by tragedies and mishaps. No, he became sturdier in his faith. He spent more time in biblical research, and prayed harder for God's mercy, grace and peace. His saddened heart was transformed into an overwhelming tide of thankfulness. For he believed that God is always good, and he trusted what God had prophesied: "All things are put together for the good of those who believe in Him."

My father was always the source of my own inspiration and encouragement. Whenever I face disappointments, difficulties, or rough corners on the road of life, I only need to look back to my father's precepts for positive answers to my problems. After the death of my second brother, who had been so wonderful, so gracious, and such a help to me, I felt profoundly lost. During World War II, every Chinese, went through unusual suffering, both spiritually and materially. Illness, material loss, and unemployment due to war conditions all converged at this critical moment. All my five children were born during the war. Bringing up babies during the uncertain days of war was unthinkably hard. No hospital, no maternity clinic, no cow's milk, canned or powdered, such as American mothers are so lucky to enjoy. To find a wet nurse was an adventure. To convince her to stay in my home and nurse the baby was as difficult as preaching to proud people. The anxiety and worry of those days sound incredible to peacetime mothers. But my parents kept up their sympathy for my inner suffering as a young mother during the horrible wartime.

My father wrote to comfort me when he and my mother were themselves grieving over family losses. One letter was as follows:

MY DEAR CHILD:

Your letter dated July 10 was received with great sympathy and understanding. We are sorry to learn that you conditions of life in this difficult wartime are so strenuous and that you suffer in so many aspects. Just think of me and your mother; our life was much harder and tougher! Your second brother was sick since January of this year, after he came back to Wuhu from the mountain of Lu. He was sick all these months, and then incurable, he departed from us...My foot being injured, I had to lie in bed for several months after your brother's death. I could not get up to walk, yet your mother and I had to bear these calamities, physical and spiritual, and learned to suppress our sorrow and to face them calmly and confidently.

I study the Bible more and more, and I pray more for God's forgiveness and consolation. I am not complaining or condemning our ill fate. I sincerely suggest, my child, that you study the Bible more, for the Bible can guide us to understand God and His will for us. Get nearer to God's side and be obedient to his command. I know that my own spiritual strength became more sturdy after facing the frequent storms of life! These are my sincere suggestions. My child, please hear my words and try to follow what I have advised.

When Generalissimo Chiang Kai-Shek was arrested by his betrayer Chang Suai-Liang, in the Si-an incident, he was prohibited from bringing any personal belongings with him, except a copy of the Bible, which he kept by his side. A newspaper has also said that in Madame Chiang's office only two things are permitted: a typewriter and a Bible. This proves that these two great persons are profoundly fond of reading the Bible. When one first reads the Bible, he often feels it to be monotonous, but if he persists in his effort and reads it regularly and seriously, he will find it an indispensable companion, and that he must read habitually. Try my advice, dear child. It is very important to put my advice into practice. Follow my biddings! Follow my bidding, my child!

Your mother and I prayed every day for you two, and the grandchildren. We pray especially for God's rich blessings upon you and your family.

FATHER, *September 1, 1944*

On January 29, 1947, my father wrote me a letter to comfort me in my distress over the frequent sickness of our two young sons:

Your letter of the 10th instant was received. Your mother and I were sorry to know that the two grandsons are very sick in the hospital. We knelt down immediately after learning this, and prayed to God for their speedy recovery. May the Holy Spirit of God comfort you and bring you happily through present afflictions. I like what you wrote in your letter: "We rely on our religious faith for a happy solution of our difficulties in life."

Remember what St. Paul says: "All things are put together for the good of those who believe in God." (Roman 8:21.)

As my children, you know very well how much distress and misery we have undergone these few years, but I adjusted to all these zigzag happenings calmly. I always meditate on what King David said in Psalm, and also in our Chinese proverb: "Submit to time and listen to what Heaven commands."

There is no use worrying as it leads to frustration and only increases one's mental burden. We Christians should endeavor to place our spiritual load in the hands of God, for God is good and merciful. He will know how to take care of us and grant us the peace which surpasses human understanding.

Philippians 5:6,7 says: "Be anxious for nothing; but in everything by prayer and supplication with thanksgiving let your requests be made known unto God."

Father's heart was enlivened by Jehovah; his spirt uplifted by God's revelation. Bitter experiences strengthened his will power, stabilized his convictions. He forgot his own pain in life, moreover, and tried to bear and to share the sorrow of others. He continued to seek righteousness and truth of God. He hoped to achieve a beautiful and good life of his own, but he was also concerned about his children, his grandchildren, and the rising generation. He hoped that all churches and mankind would unite in striving for the realization of God's kingdom on earth.

In the year 1948, on an autumn day, my father limped at slow pace, but mostly by train, from Wuhu to Nanking, one hand holding onto an old servant and the other holding a cane. Nanking was the capital of the Chinese Nationalist Government. It was a surprise visit. He wanted to see me, his tenth child, and my family in Nanking.

His visit was a surprise, but it had a divine purpose. He intended to teach his little grandchildren, four of them, aged seven, six, five, and fourteen months, Bible stories, and to recite and understand the Lord's Prayer. He taught them every evening, patiently and happily. The four little children were curious and attentive, sitting around their kind minister grandfather.

One evening during the family service, my father asked his six-year-old grandson David: "Do you know what is meant by 'Amen'?"

"It means 'finished,'" David answered with assurance. Grandfather was impressed by the answer, and though the child both wise and humorous.

He was deeply concerned about his youngest granddaughter, who was fourteen months old at that time, and had not yet been christened. It was my father's idea to come to Nanking to baptize her, so that the little soul would be purified from early infanthood by the gracious embrace of God's love and goodness.

In our home Nanking, one afternoon, my father baptized his beloved grandchild in the solemn and loving atmosphere of a family reunion. She was the last baby grandchild of my parents to be baptized by my father. He was exceedingly contented at being able to fulfill this holy duty. It was a divine and loving though for him and Mother to come to visit us.

Three days after the baptism, he left with mother for Wuhu. It was in October 1948. This was the first reunion with my aged parents after eight years of separation during World War II; it also marked the last separation between me and my beloved parents!

In the winter of 1948, the color of China changed. The Red atmosphere overwhelmed the whole landscape of the mainland of my dear China. A heavy and cold iron curtain was drawn that separated the dear parents and their daughter.

But the reunion is a deeply meaningful memory in my record of love. And in the calendar of remembrance it occupies a page of priceless significance!

A SONG OF LAMENTATION

10

ON AUGUST 8, 1951, A HOT AUTUMN MORNING, A knock sounded at our door in Hong Kong. I went to the door and found a messenger from the telegraph company. My hands were trembling as if shocked by electricity. The telegram was addressed to me. My husband opened it for me. The message was not written in words but in numbers. As he translated the last few words, my husband's face turned sad. He said hesitantly: "You father is very, very ill..." I guessed that the news must be more serious than that. My heart was bewilderingly mixed up, as if waves were whirling around in a messy chaos. I burst into sobs—spontaneous and irresistible! I grieved over the loss of my father—a great man, the kind of man most needed in an age of spiritual decadence!

My eldest brother David wrote me: "Father was going to Holy Communion Service at 9 a.m. on August 5, 1951. In the evening he felt ill, had fever and headache. At twilight, the next day, he became unconscious, and left peacefully for his heavenly home. All his loved ones knelt down beside his bed to pay him the last tribute of respect, sobbing. But when we realized that God's faithful servant had ended his strenuous journey, had calmly emancipated himself from the mortal physical shell, and had entered into the eternity of Christ to enjoy everlasting tranquility, we were comforted by the blessed privilege of being Christians. We, as Christians, should restrain ourselves from excessive grief, and should sublimate our sorrow into hopeful optimism and gratitude to God for giving us a great father, whose glorious life shall be a priceless heritage to his children and theirs..."

After completing his travel as a pilgrim, what my father has left behind to his children are neither exquisite buildings or gorgeous mansions nor a huge bank account, but the beautiful traces of his footprints on the sands of time, and his inspirational, intelligent words and exhortations—the permanent possessions and intangible properties stored in the souls of his beloved ones. His thought and deeds shall shine eternally with the sun and moon in the starry sky.

On August 7, 1952, the first anniversary of my father's death, this lament flowed from the natural spring of my affection:

One year ago of this same day

My merciful father was departing away;
Those thousands of roaring waves
And hundreds of folded hills,
Shut behind the cruel and impassable curtain of iron,
Prohibited my last gaze at him;
Nor could I offer
A bunch of fresh epidendrum
To adorn his lonely grave.
My heart is ever filled with regretful lament
Even though I hold my tears brave!

Rest thyself, my reverend father,
Casting off all earthly triviality,
Slumbering in the heavenly mansion of sweet tranquility.
What a release for you
To withdraw from quarrelsome mankind!
Though the world has been mean to you,
Yet you existence has enriched it with blessings,
Cutting away thorns and wild grass,
Creating gaiety and blissful conditions of life
For lost and forgotten souls
Out of the precious gold of your sincere and benevolent heart.

Ever since your date of departure,
Incessantly I am pondering
On your true beauty and greatness,
Which becomes my priceless compass.
Embracing your invaluable exhortations
Dare I not to tread on any rough voyage ahead?
Hear, Father,
Hear the pledge of love of your child,
Hear the praising voices,
Shall ever reach and comfort you in Heaven!

When I am struggling alone in this cruel world, I miss my father's kindness. Reflecting, I assure myself that he was emancipated from his exhausted physical self, and I feel very proud of him. More than half a century he lived an abundant and serviceable life. He gave substance to the lives of others, and filled empty and lonesome souls with God's love and purpose. For these intangible achievements, I praise him, and teach the rising generation to praise him.

The loss of my father left a brand on my heart, but it is a scar of glorious agony!

I meditate on the hymn that my father wrote in 1929, "I Am a Pilgrim Here":

I travel on the earth
Yet my home is above;
Lord often warns His children
"Be good and prepare to return."

Passing through worldly miseries,
Henceforth safely cross Jordan;
Fearless in the shadowy valley,
For I rely on Lord's rod.

As my journey ends,
Angels extend their welcome,
Jesus wipes my tears,
Comforts my contrite heart.

My head wears a royal crown,
Glorified with sublime honor,
Singing "Holy! Holy! Holy!
Praise Lord for evermore!"

Francis Bacon said in his will: "I bequeath my soul to God...my body to be buried obscurely. For my name and memory, I leave to men's charitable speeches, and to foreign nations, and the next age."

This might have been said of my father's departure, for he will be cherished in memory, generation after generation to come.

UNFINISHED CHIMES

11

AS THE STREAM OF RECOLLECTION APPROACHES ITS end, I am back in the territory of reality. Shivering as if on the brink of a precipice, my feet seem planted on the boundary between light and dark.

I open my eyes. I see a world of ugliness. The overwhelming atmosphere of materialism and Communist totalitarianism infiltrates into every walk of life. The force is as vigorous as the roaring storms of the Red Sea. The devastating picture of my homeland Sovietized—people degraded to "blue ants," harnessed like beasts of burden! Threats of annihilation are continuously being voiced by the rulers of the opposing side, while the people of this side enjoy shallow peace, living reluctantly in an unnatural state of fear and under constant challenge of nuclear war... I become uncontrollably confused and afflicted.

I feel the hostility and arrogance of humanity. Hatred exists between nations, social classes, and political parties. One race despises another race with cold prejudice. Nation fights nation with poisoned shafts. Individual segregates individual because of color, economic disparity, or class—all of which widens the spiritual distance between human hearts. Millions upon millions of people exist aimlessly in solitude, suffering the compelling inroads of hunger and exhaustion in their empty souls. Selfishness, violence, and ferocity are becoming more and more dominant in ruling the relation between men and nations. People seem to have lost their desire and enthusiasm to understand each other. Suspicion and distrust displace understanding hearts. The political dictators, because of their insatiable desire for aggression and domination, let the whole world grope in tragic perplexity and anxiety, while the invisible shafts of distrust, intolerance, and hatred are carried to the inner recesses of every phase of human life. Each blames the other as his true source of frustration; each curses the other as his master of ill fate. The God-like beauty of human nature is fading away. The original consistency, harmony, and tranquility of the globe have been smeared by the mad tyrants of power and fame. Innumerable decent homes are being split apart; millions of happy souls grope in crowded loneliness on the margin of death, sneaking and struggling for a chance to breathe free air! Communist brutality and subversion threaten the entire Eastern Hemisphere, and eventually shall spread like a plague to plunge the whole world into a ditch of tragic destruction. Oh, the whole day is as gloomy as a chilly winter day without sunshine!

Looking deeper into the heart of our society, so-called free and democratic society, in the Eastern or in the Western Hemisphere, I see growing abnormalities. Hunger, unemployment, restless wandering, economic chaos, anxiety over material insufficiency. While the other extreme of the picture shows people lolling in idle luxury, overemphasis on and concern with love of ease, acquisition of wealth as more important than the claims of family affection and real friendship. People indulge in fierce rivalries for top cash rewards and personal popularity. The growing fashion is to find satisfaction in flatteries and superficialities, and a lack of honesty and integrity tinge people's conscience. Many people spare no effort to improve themselves in intelligence and self-discipline, but people with weak willpower who feel the uncertainty of human life develop self-pity and self-indulgence. Consider the popular Chinese attitude during wartime: "Get drunk if you have sufficient wine for today, for you never can tell what will happen tomorrow; let us bear tomorrow's sorrow when it comes." Many people decline to train themselves to endure hardship, unaware that enemies lie dormant in everywhere. The ambitious money-worshipers praise the omnipotence of material wealth and chase breathlessly after vanity and fame. Many innocent youngsters fall victims to evil material and social temptations, and juvenile delinquency and other antisocial attitudes flower like bamboo shoots after spring rain. Today's so-called free society is plagued with problems that seem to defy solution. Relaxed moral standards, the growing tendency toward self-indulgence, pleasure-seeking selfishness, the alarming increase in the crime rate, the rapid spread of gambling, alcoholism, divorce, and other evils—these are the ominous signs of moral disintegration.

I observe that many families are not founded on real affection and faith but on irrational and the lower forms of marriage ideology, that is, present-day marriage is predominantly based on casual acquaintance or shallow friendship or mutual convenience or blind passionate romance rather than the solid rock of love and companionship. I have observed these changes in my homeland, in the Far East, and in foreign countries. Between husband and wife, and parents and children, there is a spiritual segregation, and commercialized affection undermines their relationships. Homes are not built on love and self-effacing cooperation. Many want to escape from home, to desert the partner who at the beginning was loved dearly and yet blindly against parental advice. The fashionable form of love nowadays is one of superficial pleasure, with no emphasis on virtue and the inherent qualities of the individuals involved. Most people marry because of money, social status, and vanity, which are no permanent possessions in life. That is why marriage can quickly arise and just as quickly disappear. Many early marriages have resulted in suicide or pathetic separation. Such families in a democratic society, lacking a warm and affectionate atmosphere, cannot help but shake the very foundations of the democratic society.

I have also observed many individuals living aimlessly, without any genuine faith to guide them toward a richer life, and without any thought of contributing anything of value toward the common good. Many individuals who once were shining examples of virtue have let themselves degenerate, and now boast of their hypocritical honesty, damaging good people by their cunning and devilish strategies. These are discouraging scenes. I am worried when I see the high ideals of democracy and freedom being obscured by the social conduct of these wicked people.

In this age of flagrant materialism, I wonder whether knowledge, science, and material things alone can solve the danger to civilization as with a magic wand. Can they alone bring order into this tangled chaos, prevent national and international catastrophes, and cure rowing social evils? Can they forestall family tragedies? Can they safeguard humanity from moral bankruptcy? The way the world goes today makes me wonder. Yet I would like to find the truth—the right key that would solve world crises and human miseries.

My thoughts flow back to my father's work and the deeds of many great men of the past and present. They strove to bring about world unity and harmony, a world of sunshine and goodness.

I recall Wordsworth's poem, "The World Is Too Much With Us."

The world is too much with us; late and soon,
Getting and spending, we lay waste our powers;
Little we see in Nature that is ours;
We have given our hearts away, a sordid boon!
The Sea that bares her bosom to the moon;
The winds that will be howling at all hours,
And are up-gathered now like sleeping flowers;
For this, for everything, we are out of tune;
It moves us not, great God!

DAVID JUAN M.D.

Wordsworth pinpoints the root of trouble of the present age. People are so absorbed in the trivialities of daily earning and spending that they are blind to the wonder of the globe which God has so graciously created. If we see the world with a poet's eye, we have the power to preserve beauty from ugliness; to seek truth against untruth; to unmask evils through God's goodness.

I miss my dear motherland as it was in old days—a land of splendid distances and vast multitudes, enchanting scenery, magnificent and brown in the north, luxuriant and green in the south, high plateaus and impassable mountains in the west and north, to the east and south of her shores embraced by great seas, her terraced hills and rivers like fabricated embroideries of marvelous design. The valleys tranquil and the lakes transparent—glittering mysteriously under the silvery autumn moon... the chorus of frogs croaking and piping in the fragrant lotus pond on cool, soothing summer nights...the green and velvet rice fields in the springtime...the prune blossoms, the epidendrums, the bamboos, and chrysanthemums that decorate four seasons with beauty...the vivid and inspiring pictures of every movement of the blue-clad farmers... the courteous ricksha men in north China... the faithful servants... their loyalty, amiability, integrity, and simplicity suggest the genuine charm of human nature. The mental and spiritual texture of these good-natured people was instilled by the teachings of Confucius, which placed loyalty, filial piety, justice, and sincerity as basic in the art of human relationships. The magnificent and gorgeous buildings conceived from the loftiest ideas and built with artistic skill, the Summer Palace, the Temple of Heaven, the Great Wall, the Porcelain Pagoda, the Forbidden City—all these were created slowly out of the constant labor and patience of the Chinese people. All these are now shut out behind the iron curtains.

The Nationalist flag, with the blue sky and white sun symbolizing freedom and unshakable truth, no longer flies over the vast spaces or streams in the winds of my motherland—a land of long history and proud cultural heritage. Today, blazing red carpets the natural delicacy of the old beauty. Laughter, humor, and wit have been displaced by tears and fears. People are dehumanized, soul-less slaves deprived of their dignity and rights as free men. The communist tyrant swarm over the beautiful countryside like busy bees, preaching their gospel of class warfare and land reform. Actually, the gospel means brutality to the blue-clad farmers, who lose their identities as individuals and become part of a gigantic labor machine. The people are now facing a life of complete regimentation and spiritual imprisonment through the so-called Commune System and brain-washing devices. The breaking up of the Chinese family system, the cruelty of splitting loved ones apart from one another, to vagabond here and there over the four seas—these things are lamentable. The Chinese people, in or out of the motherland, are now living an inner life of miserable solitude! The devastation of communist totalitarianism has provoked indisputably a roaring storm of discontent, hatred, and denunciation in the hearts of the people at home and abroad. If the dictators possessed a poet's eye and could appreciate that sunshine and light are God's gracious gifts to all men, they might not be so hostile. The world is really too much with them!

Particularly, I am deeply concerned about the old places where my father engaged in the gigantic Christian work to which he dedicated his life. His endeavor to conserve human resources, to uplift human character, to protect human dignity and to discover human talent— these are intangible. But, the places along the charming Yangtze River valley, the big and small cities, hold special meanings and memories for me, especially the three famous cities of Hupei Province—Wu-chang, Hankow, and Hanyang—the place of his origin, the place where he started his fabulous Christian work, and the place where he began his service to God by composing and translating hymns from English into Chinese, so that people could sing them in their own language and dialects and be untied through reciprocal fellowship. In the province of Kiangsi, he has left not only his footprints but also mulberry trees, pines, and bamboos, which I believe are still growing sturdily and shall never end their cycle of beauty, and the churches, their members, and the succeeding generations have deep-rooted convictions that Christ is their way to freedom and revival. Throughout Anhui Province, he left the seeds of righteousness and truth, and planted the invisible strength of democracy and freedom. The green hillsides and velvet countrysides are crowned with places of worship consecrated to the gospel of peace, the Christian schoolhouses in every small district, the bamboos, the evergreen pine trees—all these are as unchangeable as the turns of seasons. The series of exquisite and symbolic pictures of my father's constant labor of love for Christianity and his perseverance in spiritual farming will always linger in my heart as beautiful melodies.

Now, it seems to me, I suddenly hear the unfinished chimes from the church towers of my far away homeland! I listen and meditate on how my father turned every soul he contacted to the care of God! He implanted God's precepts in his children, his church members, and every member's family. Then, he let the faith grow in each one's heart like a sturdy tree. For he believed that building up the spirit of dedication to Christen faith is an everyday process, that men and women, old and young, should be inspired by Christian leaders and workers to develop broad vision, sound judgment, flexibility and variability, and an optimistic outlook, so as to face courageously all sorts of national and personal adversities and pressures. My father strove to convert individuals into Christians and their families into Christian families. Because the family is the cornerstone of society. Within the family, there must be mutual promotion of virtue and the spirit of Christians fellowship among its members, and the giving and sharing of each other's inherent qualities for the promotion of family well-being. The patriarch of each family must take a leading part in introducing basic Christian principles into daily life. He himself must set a shining example in faith and behavior in order to be a real model for his children and relatives. Thus, almost imperceptibly, other family members and the children will be influenced and directed toward the right path for a Godly life. It was always my father's belief that the Christian outlook on life must be integrated with the inner and outer life of each individual, becoming a part of the professional, economic, social, and civic activities of each individual. With this self-regulation and self-discipline, a democratic society could be built that all would hold dear. He was never unaware of the corrupt system of things, but he always hoped for the time when God's kingdom would come to remove all wicked conditions and earthly inhabitants would be under righteous rule. We shall not achieve happiness and integrity in individual life, in family life, or in the everyday human relationships of neighbor to neighbor until we discover the Divine force that lies dormant in us.

Throughout the entire course of my father's life, he sought to break through the age of darkness to one filled with light and peace. His was a beautiful answer, a great challenge to all free men.

The world now is filled with fear, hatred, anger, and brutal forces. As Jesus prophesied in Luke 21:25, 26: "There is on the earth anguish of nations, not knowing the way out because of the roaring of the sea and its agitation, while men become faint out of fear and expectation of the things coming upon the inhabited earth." Fear, anger, hatred, and brutal forces are pathetic symptoms of the world's illness. The world needs a new spiritual force to prepare it to enter an epoch of enlightenment, an advanced and democratic society of intelligent and virtuous men. There must be a movement of moral rearmament of all free men, a movement that turns away from extreme materialism to greater spirituality; to truth instead of untruth; to honesty instead of dishonesty; to good instead of evil; and to human brotherhood instead of cruel segregation. As the late Secretary of State John Foster Dulles said: "The trouble is not material... What we lack is a righteous and dynamic faith, a spiritual rebirth, a return to God and his eternal principles of truth, of justice, and rebirth must come in the heart of every average man." Our Chinese sage Confucius said: "Heaven implants virtue in us," and "I have prayed incessantly." Also, he said in his *Analects*: "He who exercises government by means of his virtue may be compared to the north polar star, which keeps its place, and all the stars turn toward it." President Wilson also stressed that "our civilization cannot survive materially unless it is redeemed spiritually. The whole world is spiritually troubled."

Indisputably, all great thinkers, philosophers, and right-thinking political leaders have proclaimed that humanity must be reorientated to God; otherwise, lasting freedom and peace will get nowhere. The marvelous technological progress that has given us atom bombs, hydrogen bombs, missiles, rockets, etc. means nothing if these forces are controlled by selfish dictators, continually exposing people to the threat of war and complete annihilation. Scientific and technological development must go hand in hand with moral control; only then can the harmony and tranquility of the world be surely maintained.

It is the greatest challenge to all free men that they must form a united front of spiritual rearmament to draw people "to good through goodness." Christianity must guide every person in the needs of this fateful period in human history; inspire each individual to share with his brethren the responsibility of building a new age filled with faith and love. Christianity must help to conserve human resources, to dig out the precious gold that God has so graciously given to each heart and found a new goal for civilization.

Let us not be afraid of the sarcasm and disdain of the fierce enemies that lie hidden everywhere in our daily lives. Let us not shirk from our divine duty as free man. We must conquer evil forces with God given wisdom, courage, and love before it is too late. The roaring tide compels us to be vigilant; we cannot sit idly by while our enemies tell their lies and lay their futile plans. We must act vigorously as Christian soldiers, break through the iron curtain, to let in sunshine and fresh air. It is through this unity of God and men that humanity shall be brought from darkness into light in the future.

Listen! Listen vigilantly to the chimes from the church towers! They are far-reaching and long-continuing!